THE LITURGY OUR LIFE

R. CLYNES, O.F.M.

The Liturgy Our Life

 St Paul Publications

Nihil obstat:

Fr. Edmund Dougan O.F.M.
Censor Librorum.
Nov. 29, 1977 Feast of All the Franciscan Saints.

Imprimi potest:

Fr. Louis Brennan O.F.M.
Minister Provincial.
Dec. 8, 1977 Feast of the Immaculate Conception.

Imprimatur:

+ Michael A. Harty
Bishop of Killaloe.
Jan. 1, 1978 Feast of the Divine Maternity.

ST PAUL PUBLICATIONS
ATHLONE IRELAND
© St Paul Publications, Athlone, 1979

Dedicated
To
The Members of the Second Order of St. Francis,
The Poor Clares,
And
In Gratitude to God
For my Golden Jubilee
In the First Order of St. Francis.

My sincere gratitude is due to Fr. Edmund Dougan O.F.M. who has rendered me untold help and advice.

BAPTISM
CONFIRMATION
PENANCE
HOLY ORDERS
MATRIMONY
ANOINTING

EUCHARIST

ADVENT
CHRISTMAS
LENT
EASTER
PASCHAL TIDE
YEARLY CYCLE

TABLE OF CONTENTS

PREFACE

In the document, 'Catechesis in our time'[1], issued from the Synod of bishops in Rome in 1977 we read: "The Church never ceases to affirm that it is the bearer of the message of salvation to all men. It is its function *to proclaim* salvation in Christ to the world and *to effect* it.

. . . In catechesis we endeavour to understand and to experience the importance of Christ in our daily lives". Further on it says: "This is another of the principal characteristics of the Church's mission: when it recalls, commemorates, and celebrates the mysteries in memory of the Lord Jesus. . . Catechesis is thus linked with the entire sacramental and liturgical life." It sums up the real object of catechesis as follows: "Knowledge of the word of God; celebration of faith in the sacraments; profession of faith in daily life."

It is clear from the above few quotations from the Synod that the Liturgy is a basic form of catechesis, embracing the Liturgy of the word and the sacramental Liturgy in its every aspect. The *Constitution on the Liturgy* says that such is its aim: "To impart an ever increasing vigour to the Christian life of the faithful"[2]. It also states: "Christ sent his apostles to preach the gospel to every creature (Liturgy of the word). . . . His purpose also was that they might accomplish the work of salvation, which they proclaimed, by means of sacrifice and sacraments, (sacramental Liturgy), around which the entire liturgical life revolves [3]... To accomplish so great a work, Christ is always present in his Church, especially in her liturgical actions"[4].

The following pages aim at giving in Part I, a general

9

conspectus of the Liturgy and in Part II applying it to daily Christian living through the Paschal Mystery. May these pages help the reader "to know you, the one true God and Jesus Christ whom you have sent" (Jn. 17:3).

Chief Documents used in footnotes:

'Mediator Dei', Christian Worship; Encyclical of Pius XII on the Liturgy. 1947. C.T.S. London. Abbreviation: M.D.

Constitution on the Sacred Liturgy. Vatican II. Abbreviation: C.L.

Constitution on the Church. Vatican II. Abbreviation: C.Ch.

Quotations from the above are from 'Vatican Council II, The Conciliar the Post-conciliar Documents, edited by Austin Flannery O.P., Dominican Publications, St. Saviour's, Dublin. Quotations from the above documents and from 'Doctrine and Life' made with the kind permission of The Editor, to whom my thanks are due.

Quotations from the above documents are indicated in the footnotes; the numbers indicate the articles of the documents.

1. Doctrine and Life, page 4, January 1978.
2. C.L. 1.
3. idem. 6.
4. idem. 7.

Part I

THE LITURGY AND YOU

1. INTRODUCTION

This title suggests some questions one could ask. What do you know about the Liturgy? What interest have you in the Liturgy? What influence has it on your Christian life and living? As a result what influence does the Liturgy exercise on your pastoral work? The answers to these and similar questions that may come to mind are answered in the very first chapter of the *Constitution on the Liturgy* of the Second Vatican Council. So the answers are not mine but those of the teaching Church. The first Chapter treats of the restoration of and participation in the Liturgy, seen as an indispensable source of the Christian Life. Education in the Liturgy is clearly a necessity.

Before dealing with these points, we must clear the ground of some wrong ideas. From the day when St. Pius X said: "The Liturgy is the indispensable source of the Christian Life"(1) to the promulgation of the *Constitution* by Vatican II, those involved in the Liturgy have been shedding the false facade built up around it, giving the impression that it was something it really was not. Many regarded it as nothing but ritual and ceremonial. Such is not the case but both these things are necessary so that the Liturgy be celebrated respectfully, devoutly and in a way becoming to so sacred a function. Liturgy is not rubrics as most people thought. Again for far too long the Liturgy was regarded as something that pertained to an elite group of clergy or laity. This was not always the case but it so happened that we did not realise its influence or its value for our supernatural life. That was just one of those accidents of history and pertains to the history of the Liturgy. It is too vast a subject to enter into here. The Liturgy is not something new and novel that has appeared overnight in the Church. Actually it is as old as Christianity itself. That is why Pius XII said: "Nothing is more urgent and so rich in hope than to call the people of God back to the substantial food of liturgical piety"(2).

Again Liturgy is not just a form of history, satisfied with teaching or recalling past events. It is drama, but drama that produces life and grace. No doubt the Liturgy does represent events of history so vividly that they appear as happening today. This is clear from the constant use of the word 'hodie' in the Liturgy. The historical aspect is the framework for the present life-giving reality. It also looks forward to the future; it is a pledge of future glory in the life to come. The Liturgy is primarily concerned with the present. It aims at bringing us divine life here and now. This it does in a sacramental manner and hence the sacramental character of the Liturgy. Many clergy, although not prejudiced, consider the Liturgy as just one among many projects that could be useful for the apostolate. Pius XI had an answer for that when he said: "People are instructed in the truths of faith far more effectively by the annual celebration of the sacred mysteries than by any official announcement of the teaching Church"(3). Pius XII wrote: "The piety which is derived from the sacred Liturgy possesses the greatest efficacy for the spiritual lives of all Christians and for the individual"(4).

Others see in the Liturgy something beautiful, but really not at all necessary. Article 10 of the *Constitution* sees much more than that in it for that article says: "The Liturgy is the summit towards which the activity of the Church is directed; at the same time the font from which all her powers flow".

So much then for what the Liturgy is not. Let us see what it really is. It is the meeting point, the point of contact between God and man through Christ our Head, here and now in the living present. This, by divine institution, is brought about by means of sensible signs which not only signify but produce supernatural realities. Contact with Christ and His redemptive work is the vital need of mankind at all times, and as the Introduction to the *Constitution* says of Liturgy: "Its object is to impart an ever increasing vigour to the Christian Life"(5). "It is the outstanding means whereby the faithful may express in their lives and manifest to others the mystery of Christ"(6). It is Christ still living on in his Church for the glory of the Father and the sanctification of men. . . "Therefore in the whole conduct of the Liturgy the Church has her divine Founder with her"(7). The *Constitution* quotes with approval twice: "The Liturgy is the summit towards which all the activity of the Church is directed. . . From the Liturgy therefore grace is poured forth upon us and the sanctification of men in Christ, and the glorification of God is achieved in the most efficacious possible way"(8). All this shows us what the restoration of the Liturgy means and aims at. If its purpose is to bring back Christ to the people, the decisive means will demand a deeper penetration into the inner spirit of liturgical life and worship. Reforms of structure can be a help but more than that is required. As Fr. Bouyer says: "Much more than any reform of the Rites (however important that may be) the future of the whole liturgical movement and the renovation of the entire Church will depend first of all on the full and practical understanding that the clergy will acquire of that basic teaching of the *Constitution* concerning the Paschal Mystery"(9). Even after the reforms, when the first fervour of the novelty is over, there is a danger that the progress will be insignificant if the real spirit behind the *Constitution* is not grasped.

Regarding the Liturgy, the words of Christ come to mind: "The Kingdom of heaven is like a treasure hidden in a field; a man has found it and hidden it again, and now, for the joy it gives him, is going home to sell all that he has and buy that field" (Matt. 13:44) and further on he says: "It is like a householder who brings forth out of his treasures, new things and old" (Matt. 13:52). Those words remind us that the Liturgy is a treasure of spirituality lost to the majority of the members of the Church. The twentieth century has seen that treasure discovered. During the past sixty years it has been slowly unfolded to us by the Church. It is not something altogether new. The Liturgy has always been there even if its value has not been appreciated for many centuries. True, efforts were made from time to time, especially from the 17th century on, to revive it but those attempts seemed to have failed because of a variety of circumstances.

It was St. Pius X, in the opening years of this century, who sowed the seed for a fresh revival. His famous words are familiar to all: "The Liturgy is the indispensable source of the Christian Life"(10). Straight away we see his ideas and aim are pastoral. That is the aspect he wished to stress. To the zeal of the Belgian Benedictine, Dom Lambert, we owe the development of this pastoral Liturgy. He summed up his hopes in two questions: "How will the Liturgy enable me to live as God wants me to live and how will it enable my people to live that same life, the life of Christ?" In these words he too is stressing the spiritual and pastoral aspects, both for the individual soul and for the people of God as a whole. He comes back to this facet of the topic again when he speaks of the education of the clergy, and he finds in the Liturgy the true source of their spiritual life and their apostolate. An interesting point in Dom Lambert's approach was that he took the Church's Liturgy as he found it. He did not attempt to reform it in any way. Attempts at reform were among the reasons why other efforts in the previous centuries had failed. Dom Lambert saw the Liturgy as the Liturgy of the Church. In it he discovered the hidden treasure. He applied it first to his own life, and then to his priestly apostolate. He never got lost in side paths, such as archeology or antiquarianism. He did not strive to put the Liturgy of the Middle Ages into the 20th century. In a word his approach was both ecclesial, pastoral and spiritual.

However, the liturgical revival was not solely the work of Dom Lambert. The German School at the Benedictine Abbey of Maria Laach added their contribution from the historical and theological aspects. The contribution of the Austrian School at Klosterneuberg under Dom Pius Parsch (an Augustinian Canon Regular) was both biblical and pastoral. France, the home of the Abbey of Solesmes and Dom Gueranger, took up the threads of renewal from both Germany and Belgium and it too stressed the pastoral aspect. Liturgical studies, seminars, and Congresses were held over the years, especially after World War II. The Holy See kept an eye on its progress and Pius XII in 1947 issued his famous encyclical, *Mediator Dei*, which, while giving the stamp of approval to the liturgical renewal, warned against certain dangers which had to be avoided. Further study and practice led to Vatican II and its *Constitution on the Sacred Liturgy*. This is in reality the fruit of sixty years of slow progress towards the ideal first laid down by Pius X in 1903. Perhaps the foregoing has been an over simplification but it is sufficient to appreciate something of the background of both *Mediator Dei* and the *Constitution*. Both of those Papal Documents open up to us the treasures that have been hidden. They require prayerful study to be able to translate them into one's own daily spiritual life. They point out to us the way we, of the 20th century, can get into contact with Christ and his redemptive and sanctifying mystery.

From the foregoing it is clear that the Liturgy can (and ought) to be studied from several points of view: (1) from the historical aspect, but this could remain purely an interesting intellectual study if one went no further, (2) from the dogmatic and theological angle which teaches us the solid foundations upon which the Liturgy is founded and develops; (3) intimately connected with this theological aspect is the biblical aspect, so often mentioned in the *Constitution*; (4) finally from the spiritual or pastoral aspect, which is the practical and concrete application of the Liturgy to one's own personal and spiritual life. This is the most important aspect. One must try to bring one's own spiritual life under the influence of the Liturgy, for this is its prime aim as the *Constitution* says: "It is the summit towards which the activity of the Church is directed and at the same time the font from which all her power flows"[11].

A point of interest here is that the personal holiness of the individual, according to God's plan, is directed to the perfection of the whole Mystical Body of Christ as St. Paul says: "To each one of us is given grace according to the measure of Christ's bestowal, for the building up of the Body of Christ" (Eph. 4:7).

The main object of the first part of this book is to give a general outline of the Liturgy in the light of the *Constitution on the Liturgy*, issued by Vatican II.

---

1. C.L. 14.
2. Letter of Pius XII, when Cardinal Secretary of State to a Liturgical Congress in Spain.
3. Encyclical of Pius XI, 'Quas Primas', The Kingship of Christ. 1925. Page 14.
4. Letter of Pius XII to Liturgical Congress in Spain.
5. C.L. 1.
6. idem 2.
7. M.D. 176, 19.
8. C.L. 10.
9. The Liturgy revived, Louis Buoyer, p. 27. Darton, Longman and Todd. 1965.
10. C.L. 14.
11. C.L. 10.

2. THE LITURGY AND SPIRITUALITY

When we speak of spirituality or the spiritual life we mean the particular way we conceive and strive to realise the ideal Christian Life. This has many aspects or approaches but all tend to and aim at the same ideal, union with God through Christ. All the means used to develop the spiritual life have the same foundations, the same principles of dogmatic, moral and ascetical theology. As Pius X pointed out, "the Liturgy is an indispensable source of the Christian Life". To understand it as such a source we must see it, not in isolation, but rather in its relation to the Divine Plan of man's redemption and sanctification. We must view it in its relationship with the Holy Trinity. This Trinitarian aspect is clearly evident e.g., in the conclusion of the majority of the liturgical Prayers: they are all addressed to the Father, through the Son, in the Holy Spirit. We find the same in the doxology of the Eucharistic Prayers.

This Trinitarian approach is evident in the Father's approach to us and ours to the Father. The source of the Liturgy is God the Father's love, who sends his Son in visible form to prove that love in word and deed. Such is the Good News of salvation, redemption and sanctification. The Liturgy is the celebration of that redemption, both in word and in action, the Liturgy of the Word and the Sacramental Liturgy.

The Liturgy is a personal meeting with God, our Father. It

is entirely theocentric or God centred. This focus is achieved in and through the Son, its Christocentric character: "No one can come to the Father but by me, I am the Way" (Jn. 14:6). The Liturgy is celebrated in the community of the Church, and this is called the ecclesial character. It is accomplished under the veil of signs and so has a sacramental character. *Mediator Dei* says: "The Liturgy is the public worship which the community of the faithful (the Church) pays to the Father through Christ" (1) and the Council adds: "The Liturgy is an exercise of the priestly office of Christ. . .(2) Christ indeed always associates the Church with himself in this great work wherein God is perfectly glorified and men are sanctified. . . Every liturgical celebration is an action of Christ, the priest, and of his Body which is the Church. . . In the Liturgy the sanctification of men is signified by signs perceptible to the senses. . . In the Liturgy God speaks to his people and Christ is still proclaiming his gospel"(3).

The role of the Holy Spirit in the Liturgy is also all-important. One has only to read the New Testament to see the role of the Holy Spirit in the life and mission of Christ himself. Christ spoke at length during the Last Supper of the role of the Spirit in his Church. He promised to send the Holy Spirit. This sending or pouring out of the Holy Spirit on the day of Pentecost constitutes the crowning work of Christ's Paschal Mystery, and the culmination of the Divine Plan of redemption, promised in the Old Testament. Pentecost is likewise the point of departure of a new era. The ancient Law of Sinai gave place to the New Law of the gospel; the ancient chosen people gave place to the new Israel, the new people of God. In a word the Holy Spirit became the soul of the Church. Under his guidance the pilgrim Church sets out on its journey to the heavenly Jerusalem, looking forward to the triumphant second coming of Christ. The Acts of the Apostles show us that the people of the infant Church were aware of the presence and the activity of the Holy Spirit in their midst. The same can be gathered from the writings of St. Paul. The *Constitution on the Liturgy*, in its opening chapter, indicates the role of the Holy Spirit from the very start. "From the side of Christ as he slept the sleep of death on the Cross there came forth the wondrous sacrament of the Church. Just as Christ was sent by the Father, so also he sent the apostles, filled with the Holy Spirit. . . His purpose was that they might accomplish the work of salvation which they had proclaimed, by means of sacrifice and sacraments, around which the entire liturgical life revolves. Thus by baptism men are plunged into the paschal mystery of Christ; they die with him, are buried with him and rise with him; they receive the spirit of adoption as sons. . . In like manner they eat of the Supper of the Lord."(4). The Fathers of the Church have seen the blood and water flowing from the side of Christ as a symbol of baptism and the eucharist, through which the Holy Spirit is given to the faithful. So in the Mass there is a fresh outpouring of the Holy Spirit. The *Constitution* also sees in the liturgical revival now taking place in the Church a movement of the Holy Spirit. The role of the Holy Spirit in the life of the Church is evident, e.g., in the epiclesis in the Eucharistic Prayers, in the invocation of the Holy Spirit in the consecratory Prefaces for the blessing of the Holy Oils, in the blessing of the baptismal Font and in the Liturgy of the sacraments. Thus we can see that in and through the Liturgy we have the continuance of Christ's redemptive work of leading us to the Father through the Son, in the Holy Spirit.

Pius XII in *Mediator Dei* (Chapter IV) explains the relationship between the Liturgy and theology, thereby showing the riches of the doctrine contained in the Liturgy. The Liturgy can become for the soul not only a school of spirituality but also a school of theology; the 'ecclesia docens'. We should also remember that (as St. Peter tells us) the Church, the new people of God, a priestly people, is a worshipping community. This reminds us of the duty of active participation in the liturgical celebrations; each one participating according to his rank or role in the Mystical Body. This point has also been explained by Pope Pius XII both in *Mediator Dei* and in his address to the Assisi Liturgical Congress. To enter into the domain of the Liturgy one must also enter into the world of the Bible, as the *Constitution* says: "Sacred Scripture is of the greatest importance in the celebration of the Liturgy"(5). In other words we must see the Liturgy within the framework of salvation-history. Salvation-history is summed up for us by St. Paul as "The Mystery of Christ", "the Mystery of the Will of God", "the Mystery hidden from eternity, now revealed in Christ". To understand the Liturgy and appreciate its value for our spiritual life, it is essential to realise that salvation-history is the Mystery of Christ in so far as everything before him tended to him and everything after him derives from him. Nothing is now left but to reproduce 'his Mystery' in men of each successive generation "until he comes". The first chapter of the *Constitution* summarises this triple era in relation to Christ and shows us that we are now living in the third era, the era when the Church carries out her mission of sanctifying men, around which "the entire liturgical life revolves". That is how we of the twentieth century can and must get in contact with Christ. It is "the concern of the Church today, to impart an ever increasing vigour to the Christian Life"(6). This great work of the Church we are told is placed within the framework of the Paschal Mystery, the very foundation of the Liturgy.

Any restoration of renewal of the Liturgy must therefore have a solid theological and biblical background. This the *Constitution* does in the opening articles. The very first thing to be noticed in those opening articles, describing the nature of the Liturgy, is that it is all placed within the framework of salvation-history and so shows a solid scriptural foundation.

Article 5 recalls the truths of Sacred Scripture that we know so well: the sending of Christ to be the Mediator between God and man. "His humanity is to be the instrument of our salvation", a humanity united to a divine person. In other words Christ is the visible intervention of God in history, making known his willingness to save and sanctify. His life and his life-work are a sacrament, in that they constitute a sign, an outward manifestation of God's love for us. Christ is thus called the sacrament of God. The article goes on to recall the wonderful works of God among the chosen people and how this was a prelude to Christ's own work, namely his Paschal Mystery. It then shows how the Church in its turn is the sacrament of Christ. Article 6 shows us how the Church was commissioned to continue the work of Christ and how it actually continues that work. This work is still in progress, (Article 7), still a reality here and now. Article 11 passes on to deal with Participation. It lays down an absolute condition, as a foundation, namely an interior spirit. Some make the mistake of thinking that the Liturgy is merely external. The truth is that it is essentially interior, but, because it is social and communal, it expresses itself exteriorly. That is why Art. 11 stresses the need for proper dispositions which in turn demand prayerful reflection, e.g., spiritual reading adapted to the various seasons. All of this demands faith. This is still more clear when one considers that all the elements that go to make up the Liturgy (sacrifice, sacraments, sacramentals, divine praise) have one thing in common: they are all signs, efficacious signs of sacred and hidden realities. Under the veil of signs, Christ's priestly power becomes a reality in the Liturgy. That is very clear from Article 7. "Every liturgical celebration is an action of Christ the priest and of his Body, the Church". So we have three participants; Christ himself, the high priest; his members, i.e., the community of the faithful here and now assembled; and thirdly, the official or ministerial priest, who acts in the name of Christ and in the power of Christ. It is not necessary to go into the distinction between the ministerial priesthood and the priesthood of the faithful. Both are involved in the Liturgy. Pius XII explains it in *Mediator Dei* (7), and article 26 of the *Constitution* says "Liturgical services are not private functions but are celebrations of the Church: they pertain to the whole Body of the Church, but they concern the individual members of the Church in different ways according to their different rank, office and activity." Such actions as making responses, standing, kneeling, singing are all linked then with participation. Articles 27-32 treat of the various aspects of this communal participation. The restoration of, and participation in, the Liturgy are not ends in themselves. Their goal is clearly expressed in article 14: *"the Liturgy is the primary and indispensable source of the Christian Life"*. Here then we come to the very essence of the Liturgy. It is life, supernatural life, it is life in Christ. Its object is to form Christ in us, thereby giving glory to God and acquiring sanctification for ourselves. All that is again stressed in article 10. The Liturgy is life, that is clear from Christ's own words: "I came that they may have life" (Jn. 10:10); "No one comes to the Father but by me" (Jn. 14:6). That too is the theology of St. Paul. The Liturgy itself states it e.g., in the second and third Eucharistic Prayers "All life, all holiness comes from you through your Son Jesus Christ". The prayer from one Sunday Mass says: "As often as these mysteries are celebrated the work of our redemption is continued". Again in a Mass of Holy Week we pray that "as we celebrate the mystery of your Son's Passion, grant that its power may transform our lives". Many other prayers found in the Liturgy proclaim the same truth. The Liturgy therefore is a present, life-giving reality, a partaking of the supernatural life, won for us by Christ in his Paschal Mystery. The other chapters of the *Constitution* deal with this point in detail as it speaks to us of the eucharist, the other sacraments, the sacramentals, divine praise and the Liturgical Year. In passing, all these aspects are not to be considered in isolation but as a sharing of the Paschal Mystery of Christ. To help in this great work the Church musters vast resources from Scripture, the teaching of tradition, and the example of the saints. Nature and grace are made to blend in beautiful harmony; the new growth of spring, the flowers of summer and the fruits of autumn, all find a place in the Liturgy. There is that continual contrast between night and day, light and darkness, death and life; all to illustrate spiritual darkness and death, spiritual light and life. From pagan customs the Church has taken (and continues to take) what is good, in order to transform and dedicate it to the service of the one true God. She has also enlisted into her service music and architecture, painting and sculpture, poetry and drama. In a word the Liturgy today is the embodiment of her spiritual activity, progress and advancement through all the ages. Thousands upon thousands have walked this path of holiness and have risen to perfect holiness in Christ. It cannot be otherwise for Christ is the centre and source of the Liturgy, the Way, the Truth and the Life. It is "with him, in him and through him" that we go to the Father. The Liturgy is the chief instrument used by the Church and her Founder, to dispense his redemptive fruits. That is why Pius XII wrote in *Mediator Dei*: "The Liturgy is no cold, lifeless representation of past events, it is Christ himself living on in his Church, still pursuing that path of boundless mercy"(8).

However we must not forget what article 9 says: "The sacred Liturgy does not exhaust the entire activity of the Church" or article 12 which tells us: "The Spiritual life is not by any means limited to participation in the Liturgy". It points out that we must pray in secret (i.e., private prayer). We must bear about in our bodies the dying of Christ, i.e., a spirit of penance and self-denial. It then states that popular devotions are to be highly commended but should harmonize with the liturgical seasons and feasts. (*Mediator Dei* dealt with this particular point in Chapter 1, Part IV).

Education is the last point in Art. 14; also the theme of articles 15-19). It is characteristic of man that he is happiest when he can remain undisturbed in his accustomed ways and his fondest wish is to remain unmolested in them. Those words are very applicable when we think of the Liturgy. We, who live in a period of change and renewal in the Church, in the Liturgy in particular, are bound to feel the effects of change and would desire to be left alone in our set ways. It is indeed difficult for older persons, who have passed most of their lives in an unchanging and apparently changeless world of religion. That might even sum up the attitude of most clergy and laity in regard to the changes and transitions they have had to go through in the past ten years. Articles 18, 19, 21 try to solve this problem. From all that has been said I think the question of education in the Liturgy is a natural conclusion. It is a must for all of us. It is not enough to say I have read the *Constitution*. It only lays down the foundations and gives guide-lines for the subsequent Congregation of Divine Worship to implement them. This implementation of the *Constitution* on the Liturgy has been going on over the years. Documents have been issued indicating how the liturgy is to be put into practice. The outstanding results have been the issue of the new Roman Missal, the Liturgy of the Hours, and the Rites for the celebration of the Sacraments. The introductory section in each case contains a mine of instruction which enables one to grasp the spirit of the new Rites of the Mass, the Office and the Sacraments. It is documents such as these that one must reflect on to grasp something of the spirit of the Liturgy and so be able to absorb them as well-springs of Christian living. Therefore we should be familiar with the many and various Decrees and Documents which have been issued in the past ten years. If we do not know them or appreciate them how are we going to make the Liturgy something living, and essentially pastoral? In this question of education I would like to mention an important point stated in article 22, which speaks of who regulates the Liturgy. It tells us that it depends solely on the authority of the Church and it adds, "no other person, even if he be a priest, may add, remove or change anything in the Liturgy on his own authority". Needless to remark this is more honoured in the breach than in the observance. Such excuses as a period of experimentation were given. The Holy See has cleared up many problems of this nature, when it stated the period of experimentation is now over. This general review of the Liturgy in the light of Chapter 1 of the *Constitution* should convince us of its pastoral and spiritual value for the lives of all the people of God, clergy and laity. It is worth noting here that, in the Documents of the Council dealing with the clergy and with Religious, stress is laid on the importance of the Liturgy. It is a subject then that deserves our serious and prayerful study. May we not sum it all up again in the words of Pius XII: "The Liturgy presents Christ to us, not only as an example for imitation, but as a teacher for us to believe, a shepherd for us to follow, an advocate who saves, the source of our holiness and the Mystical Head, whose living members we are and whose life we live" (9). Those words recall the words of St. Paul who said: "For me to live is Christ" (Phil. 1:21)

Permit me to end on a note of hope, taken from article 8: "In the earthly Liturgy we take part in, in a foretaste of that heavenly Liturgy which is celebrated in the Holy City of Jerusalem towards which we are journeying as pilgrims;... we hope for some part and fellowship with them". That too was the hope expressed by Pius XII in the conclusion of *Mediator Dei* (10).

1. M.D. 20.
2. C.L. 7.
3. idem. 33.
4. idem. 5, 6.
5. idem. 24.
6. idem. 1.
7. M.D. Chapter 3.
8. idem. 176.
9. idem. 174.
10. idem. 174.

3. THE WORD OF GOD IN THE LITURGY

It is almost impossible to understand or take an active part in the Liturgy without a knowledge of the Sacred Scriptures, above all when it is a question of the Liturgy of the Word. Liturgical piety is essentially scriptural. One has only to look through the various liturgical books to realise this. The Lectionary used at Mass is the Sacred Scriptures. The Liturgy of the Hours (Breviary) has the greater portion of its contents taken from scripture. In the new Rites for the celebration of the sacraments scripture finds a place. Also penitential Vigils are based on scripture and contain scripture readings. One cannot read the *Constitution on the Liturgy* without realising the important place it gives to the Word of God. It tells us that from the earliest days "the Church has never failed to come together to celebrate the Paschal Mystery; reading those things which were in all the scriptures concerning him". [1] Again he says: "He (Christ) is present in his word, since it is he himself who speaks when the Holy Scriptures are read in Church." [2] "Sacred Scripture is of the greatest importance in the celebration of the Liturgy. It is from Holy Scripture that lessons are read and explained in the homily and psalms are sung; the prayers, collects and liturgical songs are scriptural in their inspiration". [3]

To impress on us the value of the Word of God in the Liturgy the *Constitution* goes to tell us that: "In sacred celebrations there is to be more reading from Holy Scripture, and it is to be more varied and suitable. . . The treasures of the Bible are to be opened up more lavishly, so that richer fare may be provided for the faithful at the table of God's Word. (4) It is essential that warm and living love for Scripture be promoted." (5) Recall here what the fourth book of the imitation of Christ says about the Word of God: "Thou hast given to me thy sacred body for the nourishment of my soul and body, and set thy word as the light of my soul and thy Sacrament is the Bread of life. These also may be called the two tables, set on the one side and on the other in the storehouse of the Holy Church" (Chapter 11).

In the Liturgy, Sacred Scripture is closely linked with Christ's body. "This is the Chalice of the New Testament." Chalice and book each in its own way contain the new Covenant. In the Mass the Sacred Body of Christ is surrounded on all sides by Sacred Scripture as the royal purple. St. Hilary speaking of the Mass says: "It is from the table of the Lord that we receive our nourishment, the Bread of Life, and it is at the table from which the Sacred Scripture is read that we are nourished on the doctrine of the Lord." Truth and grace are imparted to us. This proclamation of God's word in the Liturgy is not simply a record of historical events, or a lecture in Bible History; it is the solemn proclamation, the living voice of God recalling to us the central themes of salvation. Therefore, the purpose of Scriptural Readings in the Liturgy has as its object to teach the story of salvation, its preparation, its types, its prophecies, its realisation in the life and work of Christ and its continuation in the Church. Thus, the Word of God reaches us in an authentic way, in the proclamation made by the Church in her Liturgy. Did not Christ say: "Whoever hears you, hears me and whoever hears me, hears him that sent me" (Lk. 10:16).

The Word of God—What is it? What is a *WORD*? It is the expression of our thoughts and of our will. So the Word of

God is the expression of God's thoughts and will in our regard. He speaks silently to us in all nature around us, which proclaims the glory of God. He speaks to us through the prophets in the Old Testament, and in the New Testament He speaks to us through his Son, the Eternal Word made flesh. This treasury of Christ's word he himself entrusted to his Church, and so it is she who speaks to us in his name and with his power. Hence there is a sending of the Spirit, and we must open our hearts to respond. At the Gospel of the Mass, we sign ourselves with the triple sign of the cross on the forehead, lips and heart, signifying that we wish to receive Christ's teaching into our minds, to testify to it with our lips and to cherish it in our hearts. We are listening with the ears of our body to the reader, and with the ears of our soul we are attentive to the words of him who has the words of eternal life. The Word of God then not only instructs but also has power of imparting Divine Life. "The words I have spoken to you are spirit and life" (Jn. 6:64).

St. Paul knew the value and the power of the Word of God. To his disciple Timothy he wrote: "Continue in those things which thou has learnt, because from thine infancy thou hast known the Scriptures, which can instruct thee to salvation. All Scripture, inspired by God, is profitable to teach, reprove, correct, that the man of God may be perfect in every good work" (2 Tim. 3:14-15). Elsewhere the same apostle says: "Let the Word of God dwell in you abundantly" (Col. 3:16). The Fathers of the Church see Sacred Scripture as a dynamic force, still making its impact on all who approach it with faith. It is living, active and effective, not just a souvenir from the past. "The word of God is perfect, it revives the soul" (Psalm 18). "Heaven and earth shall pass away but my word shall not pass away," said Christ (Mk. 13:31).

The Holy Scriptures give us explicit knowledge of God and his Son, Jesus Christ, a knowledge which Christ calls eternal life. Do we not speak of the Sacred Scripture as Revelation? It is God revealing himself to us; God telling us in human words about himself, his nature, his perfections, his work of salvation. The long series of revelations reaches its climax in the New Testament where we find the words of Christ himself. The Gospels are full of references to him, his person, his words, his deeds of love and mercy, his work of redemption. St. Jerome says that "to be ignorant of the Scripture is to be ignorant of Christ." The Gospels reveal Christ to us as the truth, the Divine Teacher, "I am the Truth," he said and the Father confirmed this with the words: "This is my beloved Son, hear ye him" (Matt. 17:5). St. Peter once said to Christ: "Lord, to whom shall we go, for thou hast the words of eternal life" (Jn. 6:69).

In his Epistles, St. Paul has one aim, to lead us to the knowledge of Christ, to expound the mystery of Christ. St. James says: "Receive with meekness the word planted in you, which is able to save your souls" (Jm. 1:21). The power of the Word of God was made clear by Christ himself in his parable of the sower. The seed, Christ tells us, is the Word of God and the fruit it bears will depend on the receptivity of the soil (our souls). Not only in the Liturgy of the Mass do we find the Word of God, but also in the Liturgy of the sacraments and of the Divine Office. So, too, many of the prayers and ceremonies throughout the liturgical year are rooted in scripture; e.g., the blessing of the Holy Oils, and the Baptismal Font, the Easter Vigil readings and prayers. The Council also treats of the Word of God in its decree on Divine Revelation. The early Fathers of the Church spoke frequently of the value and power of the word of God. They liked to link Sacred Scripture and the Incarnation of the Word. Through the action of the Holy Spirit in Mary, the Word of God was clothed in human nature, and through another action of the Holy Spirit in the Sacred Writers, in the womb of their intellects, the Word of God dwelt amongst us. The words of Deuteronomy: "Neither is there nor has there been any other nation that has its gods so nigh to them as our God" (4:7), are often referred to the Incarnation or to the Holy Eucharist, but the Fathers tell us that in their original context they refer to the Sacred Scripture being a sort of Incarnation of the Word of God, of the Wisdom of God.

The chosen people made this presence of God in his Word an object of reverence and worship; the tables of the Law were placed in the ark; in the synagogue the Sacred Scriptures were placed in a cupboard facing the people and no one touched the Sacred Books with unwashed hands. St. Augustine has this to say of the Word of God: "The Sacred Scriptures were written for us, preserved for us. They are recited to us and will be recited to our descendants, right to the end of time. The inspired Word of God, put into writing at a given moment, is addressed to the Church of all ages. It is an eternal present. We must listen to the Gospel as to Christ amongst us—it is the very mouth of Christ. In truth—to understand the Sacred Scriptures, what is essential is, to pray. Give me freely the time I need to meditate on the secrets of your law, reveal those pages to me."

Every heavenly reality offered us has a twofold aspect, one appearing to the senses, the other to faith. Such was the case with Christ when on this earth. His enemies, seeing with the senses, beheld in him only a man, but his followers believed in Him, and accepted Him also as God. That demanded faith on their part. The same is true in regard to the Scriptures, not everyone who reads them encounters Christ; only faith has ears to hear his voice: "My sheep hear my voice" (Jn. 10:27). Every action, every presence of Christ is a work of redemption, and Sacred Scripture is no exception. One need only recall the two disciples on the road to Emmaus, "Was not our heart burning within us, whilst he spoke in the way and opened to us the Scriptures? (Lk. 24:32). Again, one sees the power of the Word of God on the two occasions that Christ multiplied the loaves. He did so to satisfy the hunger of the multitude who had followed him for some days to listen to his words. They left their homes, they did without earthly food for the Bread of Life, the Word of God. St. Jerome says: "The Gospel is true food and true drink." When we hear or read the Word of God—"The obedience of faith"—to use a phrase of St. Paul, must be given.

In *Mediator Dei* Pius XII wrote: "In teaching us the catholic faith, in exhorting us to obey the commandments of Christ, the Church is preparing the way for her most priestly and most sanctifying action. She is also disposing us to study more closely the life of the Divine Redeemer and leading us to a deeper understanding of the mysteries of faith." [6] The same Pontiff also said: "If the liturgy communicates the truth of Christ, it is for the faithful to accept it wholeheartedly and make it a reality in their lives." St. James tells us that we must become not only hearers but also doers of the word. "Blessed are they who hear the word of God and keep it" (Lk. 11:28).

The Old Testament

We have become familiar with a triple reading in the Liturgy of the Word on Sundays. One of the readings is from the Old Testament (except in Paschal Time). This is carrying out the instructions laid down in the *Constitution on the Liturgy*. In Article 51 we read: "The treasures of the Bible are to be opened up more lavishly, so that richer fare may be provided for the faithful at the table of the Lord. In this way a more representative portion of the holy Scriptures will be read to the people in the course of a prescribed number of years." For many people the Old Testament is a closed book. It was not always so. The early Fathers clearly showed the value of the Old Testament; for example, St. Augustine says: "In the new Testament the old appears." On one occasion a child was asked at the Confirmation examination what is the Old Testament and the child responded: "The Old Testament is the life of Christ before his birth." How true that is when we recall the words of Christ himself: "You study the Scriptures, believing that in them you have eternal life; now these same Scriptures testify to me" (Jn. 5:39). On another occasion he said: "I came not to destroy the Law and the Prophets (i.e., the teaching in the Old Testament) but to fulfil them" (Matt. 5:17).

After his resurrection Christ spoke to the two disciples on the Road to Emmaus: "Beginning at Moses and all the prophets he expounded to them in all the scriptures the things that were concerning him" (Lk. 24:27). They afterwards said to one another, "were not our hearts burning within us, whilst he spoke on the way and opened to us the Scriptures?" (Lk. 24:32).

What we must not overlook is the fact that the Old Testament is also the Word of God. It is God revealing himself to his chosen people. It is salvation history. Neither must we forget that Jesus himself was trained and educated in the tradition of the Old Testament. He heard it read and explained each Sabbath in the Synagogue. His prayer life was nourished with the psalms of the Old Testament. Needless to say that Christ utilised the Old Testament to explain his mission and to show that he himself was the long-expected Messiah. He was the new Adam, the Moses of the new Covenant, the David of the new Kingdom. Many other personages of the Old Testament were figures of him in one way or another. Many of his parables have their counterpart in the Old Testament e.g., the Vineyard, the vine. He recalled God's love and mercy to the chosen people in the

34

past. The same approach was to be used by the apostles and the evangelists. Take the gospel of St. Matthew; it is full of references to the Old Testament. Christ frequently uses phrases such as: "That the scriptures might be fulfilled" (i.e., completed, perfected). The gospel of St. Matthew shows how all the prophecies were fulfilled in Christ that his gospel has been called "the gospel of fulfilment". The theme of his gospel is to show that Jesus, his doctrine, his work demonstrated that he was the Messiah. Apart from their Jewish upbringing the apostles understood that God had not two distinct messages. It was the same God who spoke to the prophets of old and who acted through the events of the history of the chosen people. All the time he was preparing them for the Word made flesh. This is clearly stated in the opening words of the epistle to the Hebrews: "God who at sundry times and in divers manners, spoke in times past to the fathers by the prophets, last of all in these days, hath spoken to us by his Son." That too is what St. Paul had in mind when he wrote to the Ephesians: "That he might make known unto us the mystery of his will" (1:9), and to Colossians: "The mystery which hath been hidden from ages and generations, but now is manifested. . . the mystery which is Christ" (1:26).

The New Testament

When we read the New Testament we must do so in the light of the Old Testament and try to get the mind and background and outlook of the writers. It is interesting to note how the *Dogmatic Constitution on the Church* refers to the close link between the Old and New Testament.

"Already from the beginning of the world the foreshadowing of the Church took place. She was prepared for in a remarkable way throughout the history of the people of Israel and by means of the Old Covenant." (7) Just as Christ was the fulfilment of his person and work of the Old Testament, so the Church sees herself as the new people of God, the new Jerusalem, the new Kingdom of God. Again the *Constitution on the Church* gives us many images of what the Church is and many of those images are taken from the Old Testament. Again in the Decrees on Divine Revelation we see the value of the Old Testament explained in Chapter IV. In the *Decree on Non-Christian Religions*, article 4, we have a clear statement on her relationship to the Old Testament; it speaks of the spiritual bond linking the people of the new Covenant with Abraham's stock. She says, "the Church cannot forget that she received the revelation of the Old Testament through the people with whom God in his inexpressible mercy deigned to establish the Ancient Covenant." Is not all this summed up for us in the 11th chapter of the letter to the Hebrews?

The *Constitution on the Liturgy* leaves us in no doubt about the value of the Old Testament, when it speaks about the Sacred Scriptures and their use in the liturgy. One has only to turn to the liturgy to see the value and importance the Church has always placed on the Old Testament. In the early centuries there was always, both in the East and in the West, a reading from the Old Testament. The former has always retained this custom. In the Roman Church it was retained on Ember Days and in Lent. It is interesting to study the passages used in our previous missal during Lent. Those Old Testament passages usually found their counterpart in the gospel readings. Many of those passages are now retained in the new Lectionary during Lent. The same pattern can now be noticed in the Old Testament Readings and the Gospel Readings on the Sundays. From a study of these Readings in the Lectionary we can learn a lot about the

Old Testament and its relationship to the New Testament.

Another important point to remember is that the Church's own official prayer, the Office, is made up of, for the greater part, the psalms. In the Mass the psalms find a place especially in the Responsorial Psalms. The Liturgy then offers us a very practical way of becoming familiar with the Old Testament. The Liturgy of the Word in the Mass gives us a clear vision of salvation-history unfolding itself to us and we can thereby realise its value from the words of St. Paul to the Romans: "What things soever were written, were written for our learning, that through the comfort of the scriptures we might have hope" (Rom. 15:4).

1. C.L. 6.
2. idem. 7.
3. idem. 24.
4. idem. 51.
5. idem. 24.
6. M.D. 38.
7. C. Ch. 2.

4. THE EUCHARISTIC LITURGY

We read in the *Constitution*: "The two parts which go to make up the Mass, namely the Liturgy of the Word and the Eucharistic Liturgy, are so closely connected with each other that they form but one single act of worship." [1] We have considered the Liturgy of the Word. We now pass on to consider the Eucharistic Liturgy.

"At the Last Supper, on the night when he was betrayed, our Saviour instituted the Eucharistic Sacrifice of his body and blood. He did this in order to perpetuate the sacrifice of the Cross. He wished to entrust to his beloved Spouse, the Church, a memorial of his death and resurrection, a sacrament of love, a bond of charity, a paschal banquet in which Christ is eaten." [2] To appreciate fully all that the holy Eucharist means to us we must go back in spirit and recall all that was said and done by Christ on that solemn occasion.

The first point noted by the evangelists is that the Holy Eucharist was instituted at the Paschal Supper, on the eve of Christ's death. Christ had not, as he had said earlier, come to destroy the law but to fulfil it, and it was within the framework of the Paschal Meal that he gave us the sacrifice of the New Law. He left his followers a memorial-rite similar to that of the former covenant which God had made with his people through Moses—that covenant which was a symbol of the new alliance which God would make through His Son. Recall the outlines of that first agreement on Sinai.

Before their liberation from the bondage of Egypt, they sacrificed the Paschal Lamb, and sprinkled the door-posts with its blood. In the third month of their journey to the Promised Land, they arrived at the foot of Mount Sinai and there God sealed his covenant with them.

We find the account given in the twenty-fourth chapter of the book of Exodus: "If you will hear my voice and keep my covenant you shall be my peculiar possession above all people. You shall be to me a priestly kingdom and a holy nation. Moses wrote the words of the Lord and taking the book of the covenant read it in the hearing of the people and they said: "All things the Lord hath spoken we will do. We will be obedient." Moses built an altar at the foot of the Mount and they offered holocausts and sacrificed victims. Moses took the blood and poured half of it on the altar. He took the other half and sprinkled the people, and he said: "This is the blood of the covenant which the Lord hath made with you." They did eat and drink. Three things go to make up the covenant; the reading of the law of the Lord, the offering of the sacrifice ʲwhich sealed the covenant and finally the eating of a meal, the symbol of the bond of unity between the Lord and his people. We know from the Old Testament that this covenant was renewed on various occasions in their history but especially each year at the festival of the Pasch with its supper. Every Jew felt he personally was involved in this great redemptive action whereby God had liberated them from slavery and made them his chosen people. To this day it is expressed in their paschal ritual: "It is not our ancestors only that the Most Holy redeemed from Egypt but us also did he redeem with them. We thank Thee, O Lord, our God, for this liberation and for the covenant which Thou hast made known to us." This paschal solemnity was for them the great annual renewal, and response to God's love for them. It was this paschal banquet that Christ and his apostles were celebrating on the first Holy Thursday evening in the upper room in

Jerusalem. Its symbolic meaning was to give place to the reality when the new covenant foretold by Jeremias was to be made and also ratified in blood.

Christ followed the three stages of the ancient covenant-ritual. First of all the promulgation of the New Law: "Little children, yet a little while I am with you. A new commandment I give unto you that you love one another as I have loved you, that you also love one another. By this shall all men know that you are my disciples, if you have love one for another" (Jn.13:33-35). The substance of the New Law is clear from the words of Christ's last discourse; namely, the commandment of love. The response must be obedience to his commandments, and the fruit of that love and loyalty will be the abiding presence of the Holy Trinity in our souls and the promise of a place in heaven. "If you know these things," said Christ, "you will be blessed if you do them" (Jn.13.17).

Then follows the sacrifice, as on Sinai, to ratify the new covenant. The Synoptics and St. Paul give us the details of this sacrifice: "While they were at Supper Jesus took bread and blessed and broke and gave to his disciples and said, 'Take you and eat, this is my body which shall be delivered for you.' Taking the chalice, he gave thanks and gave to them saying: 'drink you all of this, for this is my blood of the new Testament which shall be shed for many unto the remission of sins. This do for a commemoration of me. For as often as you shall eat this bread and drink the chalice you shall show forth the death of the Lord until he comes.' " This is the new memorial-rite whereby the new and eternal covenant is to be celebrated and perpetuated. In the Eucharist we have the real presence of Christ, the abiding love, the sacrifice of redemption and a sacred banquet.

From the Gospel description of the institution of the Holy Eucharist it is clear that Christ instituted a new Paschal Banquet in which he himself would be both the sacrificial Lamb and the food for the banquet. Saint John links the Last

Supper with the Cross, indicating that Christ crucified is the true Paschal Lamb, of whom the Baptist had said: "Behold the Lamb of God, who taketh away the sins of the world" (Jn. 1.29). Again in his opening account of the Last Supper he says: "Before the festival day of the Pasch, knowing that his hour had come that he should pass out of this world to the Father. . ." (Jn. 13:1). The Old Law was passing away and the New Law was coming into force. This covenant would be sealed in Christ's blood on the morrow. That would be his Pasch, his Passover from this world to the Father. That 'passage of the Lord' would redeem mankind from the bondage of sin. At the Last Supper Christ anticipated that historical event of his Paschal Mystery (his death and resurrection). This he did in the institution of the Eucharistic sacrifice and sacrament. In giving to his apostles, his first priests, the power of doing the very things he had just done, he was making it possible to make present in a sacramental manner, for all time, the reality of his death and resurrection. Thus the liturgical celebration of the New Testament, the New Covenant, is the Mass. The Last Supper, the Paschal Mystery and the Mass are three aspects of the one unique sacrifice of the New Law. On the Cross Christ was priest and victim in person, at the Last Supper he was priest in person but victim sacramentally, and in the Mass he is both priest and victim sacramentally. When dealing with the Mass it is essential to realise and understand that it is a sacramental sacrifice and therefore one must exclude all such things as would make it a natural sacrifice; for the sacrifice that is sacramental belongs to an order of things we could never have thought of, if it had not been revealed by Christ. Pius XII in *Mediator Dei* expresses it thus: "On the altar, by reason of the glorious condition of his humanity, the shedding of blood is no longer possible. Nevertheless, the divine wisdom has devised a way in which our Redeemer's sacrifice is marvellously shown forth by external signs symbolic of death."[3] The words of consecration make present the body alone, or the blood alone, thus mystically showing forth the actual separation as on Calvary; but there is no question of a living body being present without the blood, soul and divinity, and vice versa. We also have concrete evidence of this from the liturgy of the Mass itself. Immediately after the consecration the priest says: "Father, we celebrate the memory of Christ, your Son. We, your people and your ministers, recall his passion, his resurrection from the dead, and his ascension into glory" (E.P. 1.).

The outcome of Christ's Paschal Mystery was the redemption of mankind. He offered the sacrifice on Calvary as the sinless head of a sinful humanity. In the Mass the same sinless head and redeemed humanity, now his, and one with him, offer the sacrifice of redemption. Just as Christ's Paschal Mystery was the most perfect expression of his obedience to and love for his Father and his Father's will, so in giving us the Mass Christ has given us a means of joining with him in offering to God the very sacrifice by which we were redeemed. The Mass should be the exterior sign and expression of our interior dispositions of soul, namely the dispositions that filled the soul of Christ, obedience and love. That then is why the *Constitution on the Liturgy* insists so frequently on our active participation; we should not be present as mere strangers or spectators.

The above thoughts are fundamental for a proper understanding and appreciation of the Mass. We are the new people of God, a priestly people as Saint Peter calls us. The Mass calls for a personal response from each individual soul. It is the renewal of our covenant with God; a renewal of the bond of love and unity between ourselves and Christ and between ourselves and our fellow-members of the Mystical Body. As the *Constitution* points out: "It is from the Eucharist as from a fount that grace is poured forth upon us, and the sanctification of men in Christ and the glorification of God is achieved in the most efficacious possible way."[4]

The Royal Psalmist has expressed in the psalms the sentiments of heart that should be ours in regard to this wonderful 'Mystery of Faith'; "I will go to the altar of God;" "He hath made a remembrance of his wonderful works, being a merciful and gracious Lord;" "He hath given food to them that fear him;" "He will be mindful for ever of his covenant and will show forth to his people the power of his works;" "He hath commanded his covenant for ever;" "He hath sent redemption to his people." In the words of Christ Himself: "If thou didst but know the gift of God" (Jn.3:10), we would appreciate the wonders of the Mass and as the Council adds: "be drawn day by day into ever more perfect union with God and with each other."(5)

1. C.L. 56.
2. idem. 47.
3. M.D. 74.

4. C.L. 10.
5. idem 48.

5. THE EUCHARISTIC PRAYERS

A. INTRODUCTION

The Eucharistic Prayer is the very centre and core of the eucharistic liturgy. Historically it extends from the Preface to the beginning of the Lord's Prayer. Everything else in the Mass leads up to it or flows from it e.g., the Offertory is simply bringing the gifts for the sacrifice to the altar and pronouncing a blessing over them. It is within the Eucharistic Prayer the sacrifice is enacted. The Eucharistic Prayer has come down to us under various names; 'The breaking of Bread,' 'Eucharist,' 'The Prayer of oblation'. In the Roman Rite it has been known as 'the Canon'; from the fact that it was more or less unchanged since the seventh century. In the East it is known as the 'Anaphora'.

The Roman Rite now has four Eucharistic Prayers in the New Missal. The gospels and Saint Paul's Letter to the Corinthians are the sources for our knowledge of the holy eucharist. Both sources recall the time, place and circumstances of the institution of the eucharist. It was at the Last Supper, on the eve of his death that Christ instituted this sacramental sacrifice. We may wonder at the different accounts of the words used by Christ, as given in the New Testament. This difference arises from the differences in the liturgical practices in the various church-centres. Needless to say the rites were in existence before the gospels were written. Even today they slightly differ from the text in the old Roman Canon. In passing it may be of interest to note that in the original Aramaic or Hebrew formula the word 'body' was not used but 'flesh': "This is my flesh." Saint John in the sixth chapter of his gospel is the only one to retain the exact term used by Christ. For the Jews 'flesh and blood' are the two words used. Saint John says: "Unless you eat the flesh of the Son of Man and drink his blood you shall not have life in you. . . My flesh is meat indeed and my blood drink indeed. He that eateth my flesh and drinketh my blood abides in me and I in him. . . The Bread I shall give is my flesh for the life of the world" (Jn. 6:53-56). The word 'body' comes from the Greek.

To understand and appreciate the reality enshrined within the Eucharistic Prayer it is necessary not only to recall the Last Supper but also to understand something of the Jewish form of prayer. At the Last Supper the evangelists say: "He gave thanks." They do not give us the actual text of the words Christ used. No doubt they were the ones used and prescribed in the Jewish Liturgy for the paschal celebration or at least within that framework. Pope Paul noted in his guidelines to a commission he set up for Relations with the Jews: "To improve Jewish-Christian Relations it is important to take cognizance of those common elements of liturgical life (formula, feasts, rites, etc.), in which the bible holds an essential place." There is a special Jewish form of prayer called in Hebrew 'Berokoth,' in Greek 'Eucharistia,' meaning praise, thanksgiving. It is in reality a prayer of praise, blessing and gratitude to God for his wonderful works (the mirabilia Dei). It considers not merely his creative deeds but his special revelation of himself to the chosen people and their liberation. This form of prayer was their response to God who had personally intervened in their lives. We find this form of prayer expressed in their psalms, those inspired words which nourished their prayer-life. To praise and thanksgiving they added supplication or petition. The Jews laid great importance on prayer, especially prayer at meals. This took on a very special aspect at family meals particularly at the paschal meal. At the paschal meal the blessing of the first cup of wine was: "Blessed be thou, our God, King of the Universe, who givest us this fruit of the vine." This is the first cup mentioned by Saint Luke: "Having taken the chalice he gave thanks and said: Divide this among you, I will not drink of the fruit of the vine until the kingdom of God comes" (Lk. 22:17-18). Again at the end of the paschal meal they had what was called 'the cup of benediction' and the blessing was: "Let us give thanks to the Lord our God" and all responded: "Blessed be he whose generosity has given us food and whose kindness has given us life." This was followed by a series of thanksgivings (berokoth), usually three. The first was a prayer of praise and thanks for nourishment received from God. Then a prayer of thanks for all creation and for life itself (they prayed for a blessing for the covenant and the Law of the Lord). The final prayer was that the redemptive action of God in earlier times (the Exodus) be renewed and find fulfilment in the coming of the Messiah. In this prayer there is frequent use of the words 'memorial', 'remembrance': implying a sense of continuity. Those words occur six times. This shows they regarded the paschal meal as having a sacrificial character. The out-standing aspects then of the Last Supper were the prayers of praise and thanks and the prayer of remembrance. These are still outlined for us in the accounts of the institution of the Eucharist, which word means thanksgiving.

It is with this biblical background we should recall the details of the Last Supper, which gave us the new eternal covenant, renewed each time in the Eucharistic Prayer of the Mass. It is clear from the *Acts of the Apostles* that the Apostles carried out the command of Christ, given them at the Last Supper, "Do this in memory of me." This they did within the framework of a Jewish community meal and its liturgy. From the start then the influence of the Jewish Liturgy is evident. It also made itself felt in the writings of the apostles, especially Saints John and Paul. We also find traces of it in the prayers of the early martyr Saint Polycarp. The Christian communities first celebrated the eucharist in the homes of the faithful but later, when their number increased, they celebrated in a hall. It was around this period that the meal was dropped and the eucharist became a service in itself. At this period also the practice was to celebrate the eucharist on a fixed day, Sunday morning. It is in the time of Saint Justin (150) that we find the oldest account of the manner of celebrating. It consisted of readings from the prophets and the apostles (old and new Testaments) followed by a homily and prayers (prayers of the faithful). This form of service was taken over from the Jewish liturgy. Then followed the eucharistic liturgy: "The bread and wine mixed with water are brought to the president and he offers up prayers of thanksgiving, as much as in him lies and the people chime in with Amen, Amen." We see that there is no prescribed text. Up to the end of the third century there was no fixed text but in the fourth century, with greater organisation, and the influence of the large patriarchal Sees, a fixed form began to emerge around those Sees, and this development continued on into the sixth century, the time of Gregory the Great. The outcome of all this development was the five basic Rites. In the West, there was the Roman, the Gallican and Mozarabic (Spanish) and in the East, East and West Syrian and Alexandrian. This division is not watertight because each had an influence on the others. As a deeper study of all those Rites and their development is a vast subject in itself, we will confine ourselves to the Roman Rite.

B. THE PREFACE

Historically the Preface is part of the Eucharistic Prayer. The introduction of the Sanctus (both in the East and West) broke the sequence of the Prayer and the original introduction became more or less separate and was regarded as a preface in the ordinary use of the word. However, originally the Eucharistic Prayer was undivided and was known as "Praefatio" from the Latin words: "Praefari," meaning a speech or a proclamation made before an assembly or deity. From what we know of the Jewish form of prayer, the Preface highlights the duty of praise and thanksgiving and the reasons for them. It opens as a dialogue between priest and people. First of all a greeting: "The Lord be with you," which is semitic in origin. Then an exhortation (sursum corda, Lift up your hearts) and finally an invitation to give praise and thanks. This theme is then taken up and developed by the priest. Notice that the entire Prayer is addressed to God, the Father, the Lord, the Almighty, the eternal God; all terms found in the Old Testament to designate God. In the Eastern liturgies the themes of thanksgiving are manifold and extensive (as can be seen from many ancient ones which have survived). In the Roman Rite those themes are more condensed and divided up according to the various seasons and feasts. In the middle ages we do find a large number of Prefaces, often one for each Mass. The Council of Trent reduced them to about eight. Some few more were added in this century. The new Roman Missal (as a result of the *Constitution on the Liturgy*) has over eighty Prefaces and so not only gives variety, but brings to our minds the manifold reasons why we should praise and thank our God and Father. If the variable parts of the Prefaces were joined, one would have a clear picture of salvation-history.

The Advent Prefaces scan the whole of the Old Testament, sounding the note of joy and hope in the coming of the Saviour, and hoping he will welcome us when he comes again in glory. The Christmas Prefaces are linked with the prologue of Saint John's gospel; we see God made visible, we recognise in Christ his love for us. His coming is to lead mankind from exile into God's heavenly kingdom. His divine mission is again outlined in the Preface for the Annunciation; which tells us that in his coming the promises made to Israel would come true and man's hope of redemption would be realised beyond all expectation. The Lenten Prefaces are paschal in their themes. They speak of Lent as the season of renewal, of self-denial, of growth in holiness. The theme of his sufferings and death to be followed by his resurrection are placed before us in the last week of Lent. The Prefaces for Eastertide centre our thoughts on the wonders of the paschal mystery, Christ's victory and triumph over sin and Satan and our rising to a new life in him. At the Ascension we are reminded that Jesus, the King of glory, the conqueror of sin and death has ascended into heaven and that where he is we hope to follow. Pentecost celebrates the beginning of the Church and the sending of the Holy Spirit to its members. There are eight Prefaces for the ordinary Sundays of the Year and they too keep the outstanding events of salvation-history before us. So also do the weekday Prefaces for the same period. Our Blessed Lady's role in the work of salvation is made clear in the Prefaces for her feasts. The apostles have two Prefaces, one telling us how they are the shepherds of their flocks and the other that the Church was established on them as its foundation. The new Missal does not stop here, it takes up the saints and sees in them a further cause for gratitude to God. The saints extol the glory of God and they are given us as patterns and as intercessors: such witnesses should inspire us. In a Preface for martyrs the power of God is revealed, for he strengthens our weakness to bear witness even to the shedding of blood.

The Preface for religious stresses their total dedication of themselves for the sake of the kingdom of heaven. A series of five Prefaces for the Dead concludes the list. They point out the Christian theology of death and future resurrection. We can see from this very brief summary how the various Prefaces are sublime hymns of praise and thanksgiving for the wonderful works of God (mirabilia Dei) accomplished in the story of salvation-history, and this both in the Head, Christ, and in his members. Those wonderful expressions of gratitude should stir up constant thankfulness in our own hearts and be a source of encouragement in our living the paschal mystery in our own lives. Furthermore the Prefaces remind us of the doctrine of the Communion of Saints, for at the end of each we beg to unite our praise with the Church Triumphant, with the angelic choirs in their canticle of "Holy, Holy, Holy Lord".

C. EUCHARISTIC PRAYER 1

The first of the four Eucharistic Prayers in the new Missal is the old Roman Canon, with some few adaptations. This Prayer is truly Roman in its style, its sobriety of expression, its brevity and its balanced structure. We can trace the Prayer back to at least the fourth century. Originally it was in Greek but was translated into Latin by Pope Damasus. Additions were made by Popes Leo, Gelasius and Gregory, these we will note as we meet them.

The transition from the Preface (which we saw is part of the Eucharistic Prayer) is made by the words "Te igitur". This is a phrase found in the blessing of the font, oil etc., in the old missal and pontifical. "Igitur" means 'Therefore' or 'wherefore' and it refers back to the Preface. In Jewish prayer, from thanksgiving one passes on to petition; e.g., "Because of your goodness we thank you and we therefore now ask you." So the Roman Prayer begs the Father to accept and bless our gifts.

Now we find the first of the additions, namely, intercessions for the Pope, bishop, all true believers in the catholic and apostolic faith. Next comes intercessions for the faithful, those present, those who offer the sacrifice and those for whom it is offered. Those intercessions were introduced at this point as soon as they were dropped after the gospel, i.e., around the end of the fourth century. Next comes the intercession of the saints, to whom we pray that by their prayers and merits we may be guarded. The list of saints, especially of the martyrs, shows the Roman origin of this list. Another variable intercession (Hanc igitur) was inserted on certain occasions, such as baptism or ordination. Pope Gregory made it permanent, using it as a prayer for peace. In both the old and new missals special variations of this prayer are used for special occasions. Now the original prayer continues (Quam oblationem) in which we once more beg God to bless and consecrate our offering so that it may become the body and blood of Christ. Some authors wish to see in this prayer an invocation of the Holy Spirit, a Roman epiclesis, but this is not certain. As the priest recites this prayer he places his hands over the oblation. It recalls the laying on of hands on the victim by the priest in the sacrifice of atonement in the Old Law. As it then symbolised the transmission of the sins of the people to the victim immolated for their sins, so now, in the great sacrifice of the New Law, it symbolises the truth that Christ has taken upon himself the iniquities of us all, that he was immolated on the altar of the Cross for our salvation. It is a silent call to us also to die to sin. His sacrifice was not unto death but unto life, and our death to sin will lead to divine life in him.

Now comes the institution narrative, the liturgical proclamation, with the words of consecration as its heart and core. The details in word and action of what Christ did and said at the Last Supper are re-enacted. The result is the victim of Calvary, now in his glorious state, is present on the altar. The words "mystery of faith" are taken out of the wording for the consecration of the chalice and added afterwards with an acclamation from the people, professing their faith in the mystery.

There follows what is known in all liturgies as the 'anamnesis', i.e., the prayer of offering. This prayer is inspired by the command of Christ: "Do this in memory of me." It is addressed to the Father in the name of the ministers around the altar and the holy people of God present. We make a return to God of the gift he gave us, his beloved Son. In a word we offer Christ's paschal mystery. The prayer expands on and begs God to accept our offering as of old he accepted the sacrifices of Abel, Abraham and Melchisedech. The example of these three ancient sacrifices are set before us so that we may have sentiments similar to these three personages. The Prayer continues with a petition that our gifts be borne to heaven, and a plea that all who receive this most sacred body and blood may be filled with every blessing and grace. This petition is somewhat similar to the epiclesis found in the other three Eucharistic Prayers also placed after the consecration. It is a petition for the fruitful reception of Holy Communion.

Once more another twofold intercession is inserted; the Memento for the Dead and a prayer for ourselves, sinners, that through the intercession of the saints and God's mercy we may be admitted to their company. This intercession was introduced by Pope Gelasius at the same time as the intercession of the saints that follows the Memento for the living. Again one notices that the list of saints is Roman. The next few lines are a remnant of a blessing that took place at this point in the earlier centuries, a blessing of the gifts of the faithful but not actually used in the sacrifice. Those gifts were usually bread, wine, oil. They were set aside and later distributed to the poor. Some of the Holy Oils are blessed at this point on Holy Thursday. All four Eucharistic Prayers conclude with the final doxology, based on words from St. Paul (Rom. 11:36, Eph. 3:21): "Through him" etc. We pray through him who is our Mediator, for "we have an advocate with the Father," says Saint John; we pray with him, who is our Brother, "We are and are called sons of God," says the same Saint John, he by nature, we by adoption; we pray in him, who is our Head, for we constitute one Body, and so we can have unbounded confidence in his superabundant merits. The response of the faithful is the great "Amen". It is their ratification of all that has been done at the altar of sacrifice. It is not only our approval but also our commitment to live our lives in the spirit of that sacrifice.

D. EUCHARISTIC PRAYERS 2 AND 3

The second Eucharistic Prayer is based on the famous one composed by Hypolitus of Rome (early 3rd century). There has been a great deal of controversy about the original text. It now seems that it was not originally composed by him in Rome but brought by him from the East, and that he tried to popularise it in Rome. Its value lies in the fact that it is the most ancient text extant from Rome. In the original text there is no 'Sanctus'. Otherwise it follows the normal pattern of praise, thanksgiving, institution narrative, anamnesis, epiclesis and doxology. The new Eucharistic Prayer composed from it inserts the 'Sanctus' and a few other minor points considered necessary. It has its own Preface and in the new text the translation from the Preface is made by an invocation to the God of all holiness (Vere sanctus es). This form of transition is common in all Eastern liturgies.

Then comes the invocation to the Holy Spirit to effect the consecration. Notice the Trinitarian approach. This invocation of the Holy Spirit, known as the 'epiclesis' is one of the famous controversial aspects in the Mass. The controversial point is whether the consecration is effected by the actual words of consecration alone, or whether the invocation of the Holy Spirit is essential. The question has never been solved and is purely theoretical. In the original text of Hypolitus this invocation comes after the consecration. In the new text it is divided, some before and some after the consecration. This brings it into line with the Roman Eucharistic Prayer, which expresses the twofold idea but without mention of the Holy Spirit. This invocation of the Holy Spirit has almost always found a place in the oriental liturgies.

The text of the Prayer then moves on rather quickly to the institution narrative and is followed by the 'anamnesis' i.e., the prayer of offering. It also contains words of thanks. "We thank you for counting us worthy to stand in your presence and serve you." Next comes the second part of the epiclesis, again an invocation to the Holy Spirit for a fruitful communion and for unity not only with Christ but with one another, the eucharist being the sacrament of unity. It is at this point, as in all Eastern liturgies, that the prayers of intercession are said. They are not however in the original text of Hypolitus. Notice the order: the Church, the Pope, the bishop, the clergy, the dead and finally ourselves, the faithful. We pray that we may be worthy to share eternal life with Mary, the apostles and all the saints. Finally comes the doxology as in all eucharistic prayers. What conclusion can we draw from this review of the second Eucharistic Prayer? No doubt it is short, but analysis shows that it is ancient in its source and contains all the elements we are familiar with in the Roman Prayer except that the order is not the same. It is biblical and theological and brings home to us that we are praying with words that were used at Mass in the third century. What a wonderful link that is.

The third Eucharistic Prayer is a modern composition but its sources are ancient. It is modelled on Gallican and Mozarabic (Spanish) Eucharistic Prayers. This is clear from the fact that the intercessions are placed at the end. We saw that in the Roman Prayer they are divided into two, before and two after the consecration, and they tend to break the original flow of the Prayer. This third Prayer has no special Preface of its own. Once more the transition from the Preface-Sanctus (called in the Gallican Rite the Pre-Sanctus and then the Post Sanctus) is made with words similar to those in the second Prayer: "Father you are holy indeed (Vere sanctus es). It returns then to the theme of the Preface, thanksgiving: "All creation rightly gives you praise." This is done for two reasons, because "all life, all holiness comes from you through your Son, Jesus Christ, by the working of the Holy Spirit" (the Trinitarian approach). It speaks of the people of all ages and all climes being made holy and who offer a perfect sacrifice to God's name. It is thus recalling (and this is clearer in the Latin text) the prophecy of Malachy, who speaks of "the clean oblation which is offered from the rising of the sun to its setting". This idea is often found in Eastern liturgies. We then offer our gifts (bread and wine) and ask that they be made holy (consecrated) by the power of the Holy Spirit. This is the first epiclesis. Then follows the institution narrative. The words of Saint Paul are used: "On the night he was betrayed." Again this phrase is common to Eastern and Gallican liturgies. The anamnesis, called in the Gallican Rite, the Post-Sanctus, follows as in all Rites, East and West. After mention of the Ascension into heaven, it asks that we be ready to greet him when he comes again. This mention of the final coming is found in all Rites except the Roman. It makes explicit the offering of the holy and living sacrifice, and asks the Father to accept the Church's offering; the offering of herself and the Victim, whose death won our redemption. As in the second Prayer, it begs for a fruitful communion and for unity in Christ. This is the second epiclesis, as it is called. The Prayer continues on into the intercessions. The order is different from the second Prayer. First comes the invocation of the saints to share in their inheritance. Next comes the Church, a pilgrim Church, with its Head the Pope, the bishop, the clergy and the entire people of God. It then turns to the Church Suffering in a Memento for the dead. It has a special Memento when the Mass is offered for a specific deceased person. It develops the theme of the paschal mystery in the individual soul. Dead to sin with Christ, risen with Christ (in baptism), the final rising with Christ at the last day. It gives us a glimpse of the glory of heaven: we shall see God as he is and continue to give him glory through Jesus Christ our Lord. No doubt there is a depth of meaning in this third Eucharistic Prayer.

We cannot but conclude that these two new Eucharistic Prayers have enriched the Roman Rite. They are ancient and yet modern; ancient in so far as they have their source in the tradition of many ancient Eucharistic Prayers and are drawn from a storehouse of rich variety adapted to modern needs. May we not say it is once more a reminder of the gospel parables of the treasures hidden in the field and of the householder who brings forth out of his treasures new things and old? They link us with the past, we feel we are praying with past generations, back as far as the third century. They no doubt fulfil the requirements laid down in the *Constitution on the Liturgy*, about revising the Rite of the Mass that the purpose of its several parts may be more clearly manifest and the devout and active participation by the people may be more easily achieved. It also fulfils the wish that tradition be retained. They should be to us (like the Roman Canon) sacred and venerable texts which enshrine the Eucharistic mystery.

E. EUCHARISTIC PRAYER 4

This Eucharistic Prayer is unique in certain ways. It has an invariable Preface, which must always be used. This Prayer may not be used on days when a feast has its own proper Preface. However it may be used in the seasons of Advent, Lent and Paschal Time. An interesting aspect of this Eucharistic Prayer is that it is based not only on the oriental style but also on the ancient Jewish Blessing, mentioned earlier. It is a summary of salvation-history, knowing that it has found fulfilment in Christ and in his Church. It is to be noted also that the general theme of praise and thanksgiving is continued from the Preface to the end of the Prayer. On close examination one will see that the Preface concentrates on God, our Father, in himself. He is praised and worshipped for what he is and as the Creator. We praise the transcendent God who has actually made himself known above all in his creation. This leads on to the 'Sanctus', joining the angelic world and the world of men. After the 'Sanctus' it once more takes up the theme of the creation of man, God's goodness and his love. It then recalls the fall of man and his restoration in Christ. In a word it reviews God's dealings with man in the Old and New Testaments, through Christ and the Holy Spirit and so on into the life of the Church. Such is the general theme, all indeed worthy of our praise and gratitude. The 'Gloria' of the Mass summarises it all. Let us look at it in more detail. The Preface deals with praise of God before the history of salvation but it is linked with the latter in so far as both are pre-ordained to the glory of God, as Saint Paul points out. That God is worthy of praise is clear from the words: "You alone are God, living and true, through all eternity." The Hebrews, as we know from the psalms, had a vision of God as of incomparable greatness and majesty and so they felt in awe of his majesty (cfr. the vision of Isaiah 6). The Latin text brings out this more clearly (Unus es Deus, vivus et verus, qui es ante saecula ac permanens in aeternum). The Preface then passes on to recall the wonderful work of creation: "Source of life and goodness, you have created all things." Creation was the outcome of love and by responding to that love man would one day share in the joyful vision of that God of love. The Universe responds in its silent tribute to its Creator as the psalmist says: "The heavens proclaim the glory of God" (Ps. 18). We are transported to the world of celestial creatures, the world of the angels, who always stand before his presence, and we beg to unite our voices with their canticle of "Holy, Holy, Holy Lord".

This canticle of praise is continued after the 'Sanctus'. It first of all summarises all that was said in the Preface: "Father we acknowledge your greatness, all your actions (creation) show your wisdom and love." We then pass on to the story of the creation of man, "whom you formed in your own likeness," making him ruler of all creation. Saint Paul mentions this gradation in the scale of creation: "All are yours, and you are Christ's and Christ is God's" (1 Cor. 3:22-23). Yet despite his disobedience, his fall, and the subsequent loss of the friendship of God, "you did not abandon him to the power of death" (to the eternal slavery of sin and death). Rather the plan of God for the restoration of man is revealed, bit by bit, in the covenants, in the messages of the prophets, all teaching mankind to hope for deliverance and salvation. The opening lines of the letter to the Hebrews speaks of this.

Such then were the divine interventions on man's behalf. Despite all God's love, especially for his chosen people, they failed him over and over again. Then God announced that he would establish a new covenant, a covenant that would include all nations. The Prayer proceeds to praise God for sending his Son, born of the Virgin Mary by the power of the Holy Spirit, to be the 'Salvator mundi', the Saviour of mankind. This Son fulfilled all the messianic prophecies concerning him. "In fulfilment of your will he gave himself up to death but by rising from the dead he restored life." This phrase is found in Saint Paul and in the Easter Preface. "He sent the Holy Spirit from you, Father," to continue his work of restoration through the sacramental renewal of his Paschal Mystery. We beg this Holy Spirit to sanctify our gifts that they may become the body and blood of Christ, as we celebrate the new covenant. We can see the Trinitarian structure of the divine economy of salvation. The institution narrative is high-lighted by sentences from Saint John, which creates the atmosphere of the Last Supper.

After the consecration the outline is more or less the same as in the third Eucharistic Prayer. The intercessions come last as in the Jewish and oriental liturgies. We pray in this order: The Church Militant, the Church Suffering and the Church Triumphant. We pray that we may enter that kingdom of the elect to sing your glory through Christ our Lord. It is through him you have given us everything and now through him, with him, and in him, we render you, almighty Father, all honour and glory. If asked what is the basis of this Eucharistic Prayer, we must say it is love, God's undying love for us. The Paschal Mystery (renewed in the Mass) is a constant reminder of that everlasting love of God for us. Of this great mystery Christ would say to us what he said to the woman at the Well of Jacob: "If you did but know the gift of God" (Jn. 3:10).

The concrete expression of God's love for us is amply proved in the sending of his beloved Son to re-instate us as his children. The working out of this reunion constitutes what is called salvation-history. It has a double aspect. The first is viewed from God's angle, a mission of love. This coming of the God-man involved on his part a total surrender of himself to the Father's will, to his plan "to restore all things in Christ". The Incarnate Son of God makes that surrender by offering his life in sacrifice on the cross and returning to the Father through a real death, which led him however to his resurrection and ascension. That is what we call Christ's Paschal Mystery. The second aspect centres on man. Man is expected to make a response to God's love. God wishes man to accept willingly the treaty signed in the blood of his Son. The glorious risen Christ now communicates, essentially through the Liturgy and in particular in the sacraments and sacrifice, a sharing in this divine life. The fulness of divine life was first communicated by the eternal Word to the humanity of Christ at the moment of the Incarnation and is now imparted to us by Christ. "This humanity has become the instrument of our salvation." So Christ's Paschal Mystery is still present and active. It now becomes our Paschal Mystery, making us pass from death (the death of sin) to a new life, a sharing in the divine life on earth and later in the glory of heaven. We become heirs with Christ. This has been outlined for us in the first Chapter of the *Constitution on the Sacred Liturgy*: "He (Christ) achieved his task principally by the Paschal Mystery of his blessed passion, resurrection from the dead and glorious ascension, whereby "dying he destroyed our death and rising restored our life." [1] This is treated of over and over again in the writings of Saint Paul.

---

1. C.L. 5

6. THE PASCHAL MYSTERY IN THE LITURGY

Since the Liturgy is set within the framework of salvation-history, it gives prominence to the Paschal Mystery. To have a full picture of the mystery of Christ, as Saint Paul calls it, one must view it in its three-fold dimension; its foreshadowing in the Old Testament, its reality in Christ through the Liturgy.

1) The *Constitution on the Sacred Liturgy* speaks of "the wonderful works of God among the people of the Old Testament were but a prelude to the work of Christ."(1) In the light of the New Testament we now see more clearly some of those wonderful works of God. The most outstanding was the liberation of his people from the slavery of Egypt under the leadership of Moses. The Exodus led to the birth of a new people, the people of God, a holy nation. We are familiar with the events of the Exodus, the sacrifice of the lamb, the liberation from Egypt and the covenant at Sinai, all no doubt symbols of Christ's own Paschal Mystery. This latter in its turn was the symbol and reality of another liberation, that of mankind from the slavery of sin and Satan. The chosen people kept and still keep two festivals recalling those events, the feast of the Pasch and that of the Pentecost. It is for them more than a mere recalling of historical events. It is regarded a re-living, a renewal of the spirit

which animated their forefathers. Needless to say there were many other events and personages in the Old Testament which were to find their reality in the person, the teaching, the mission and the sacrifice of Christ. That is our interest in the Old Testament, and Saint Paul has two remarks to make about it: of the people themselves he says: "With many of them God was not well pleased" (1 Cor. 10:5) and again "whatsoever was written was written for our instruction" (Rom. 15:4). The Old Testament forms the initial chapters of salvation-history.

2)   When we turn to the New Testament we find the fulfilment of all the symbols in Christ. The *Constitution* clearly tells us: "Christ achieved his task principally by the Paschal Mystery of his blessed passion, resurrection from the dead and glorious ascension." [2] He is the true Paschal Lamb. In reading the New Testament we notice that Christ always linked his death with his resurrection. It was at the celebration of the Jewish Paschal Feast that he instituted the Pasch of the New Covenant, which would renew for all time his own Paschal Mystery. We see also that Saint Paul and also Saint Peter likewise link the two events that go to make up Christ's own Paschal Mystery. The Paschal Mystery is the mystery that Saint Paul speaks about, a mystery hidden in God but now revealed in all its fulness in the death and resurrection of Christ. Saint Paul sees it as the mystery of redemption.

3)   The Church is paschal in its programme, in its apostolate, especially in its liturgy, both the liturgy of the word and the sacramental liturgy. This is clearly stated in the *Constitution*: "The liturgy is the summit towards which the activity of the Church is directed: at the same time it is the font from which all her powers flow, [3] . . . For members of the faithful the Liturgy of the sacraments and sacramentals sanctifies almost every event in their lives; they are given

access to the stream of divine grace which flows from the Paschal Mystery, the font from which they draw their power."(4) A subsequent *Instruction* affirms the absolute predominence of the Paschal Mystery in Christian living. So Christians must express the Paschal Mystery in their own lives, for it is the very heart of the Christian life. We know from the gospels that Christ lived his mystery (in its various aspects) for us: "I came that they may have life" (Jn. 10:10). He offered himself as a teacher and a model. Saint Paul told us: "God chose us in Christ that we should be holy" (Eph. 1:4). It is, as we saw, the Liturgy that puts us in contact with Christ, for "the liturgy is the exercise of the priestly office of Christ. . . In the Liturgy the sanctification of man is effected." (5) "The Liturgy is the outstanding means whereby the faithful may express in their lives and manifest to others the mystery of Christ." (6) "Once a year," says the *Constitution*, "by the most solemn festival of the Pasch, the Church celebrates his resurrection together with his blessed passion." (7) We are familiar with this annual celebration during Holy Week, when the Church places before us not only in words but with all the expressiveness of her sublime and dramatic ceremonial the events of Christ's Paschal Mystery. She relives in every detail the Paschal Mystery and invites us to share intimately in it. It is not necessary to go into details beyond saying that its celebration goes back to apostolic times, thereby making clear to us the mind of the Church from the very start on this annual celebration.

4) However this is not the only celebration. The *Constitution* in Chapter 2 says: "On the night before he suffered Christ instituted the eucharistic sacrifice of his body and blood. He did this in order to perpetuate the sacrifice of the Cross throughout the centuries until he should come again; he wished to entrust to his beloved Spouse, the Church, a memorial of his death and resurrection, a sacrament of love, a paschal banquet." (8) In the Mass then we have the fountain

from which all our liturgy flows. The Church is the new people of God, the Mass is the new covenant-sacrifice of the New Law; it is the Christian Pasch. The Hebrew paschal rite prolonged the Exodus in time. Likewise Christ instituted a paschal rite to recall, and renew his Passover, his Pasch. He did so within the frame-work of the Jewish paschal rite. In that rite we find three essential elements of the original pasch, the word of God, the immolation and the supper of the lamb. Following this pattern, Christ proclaimed the New Law in his last discourse, blessed the bread and wine, changed them into his body and blood and gave them to his apostles to eat. That he wished them to renew this paschal rite is clear from his command: "Do this in memory of me; as often as you do these things you will show forth the death of the Lord until he comes." Such is the manner of the renewal of Christ's Paschal Mystery. That was his parting gift to his Church and has now become the Church's sacrifice, the one and only sacrifice of the New Law, identical with his own historical sacrifice on Calvary. That is the heritage handed down to us in the Mass. The Mass follows the same pattern. After the Introductory Rite, we have the Liturgy of the Word. In the eucharistic liturgy the offering of the sacrifice of the New Law is accomplished and the sacred banquet of the immaculate Lamb is in the Communion Rite. The fourth eucharistic prayer is not only a summary of salvation-history but it clearly places the Mass within the context of the Paschal Mystery. Every Mass mentions the paschal aspect in the first prayer after the consecration. Is it any wonder then that the *Constitution* calls for active participation of the faithful in the Mass? (9) All this is gone into in greater detail in the second Chapter of the *Constitution*.

5) The third Chapter treats of the other sacraments and of the Paschal Mystery. All the sacraments have their origin in the priestly sacrifice of Christ, his Paschal Mystery. Each

sacrament pours out the fruits of his Paschal Mystery. It is Christ entering into our lives to enable us to share it. The *Constitution* points this out when it says: "The purpose of the sacraments is to sanctify men and give worship to God. They not only presuppose faith but they nourish, strengthen and express it. . . They have power to impart grace. . . They give access to the stream of divine grace which flows from the Paschal Mystery of the passion, death and resurrection of Christ, the font from which all the sacraments draw their power." (10) The first thing the *Constitution* draws our attention to is not the administration or reception but their celebration. In other words they are liturgical celebrations, acts of worship and efficacious signs of sanctification. Since the eucharist is the renewal of the Paschal Mystery there is a close link between it and the other sacraments. This is now clear from the fact that all the sacraments (except penance) are now normally celebrated within the Mass. Penance too has its link with the Mass, more evidently in the ancient Mass of the Reconciliation of Penitents on Holy Thursday. It is also evident from the fact that people in serious sin are excluded from participation in the eucharistic banquet until they have obtained absolution in the sacrament of Penance. Baptism is very closely linked with the Paschal Mystery. Indeed this sacrament is our own paschal mystery, and Saint Paul deals with this at great length. It is also clear from the liturgy of the Paschal Vigil. Confirmation completes the grace of Baptism. Baptism, Confirmation and the Eucharist are known as the sacraments of Christian initiation. The sacrament of Holy Orders is most closely bound up with Calvary and the eucharist. This sacrament transmits power to others. The sacrament of the sick unites the sick person with the suffering Christ and his merits strengthen the soul and body of the one who receives this sacrament. Matrimony draws its inspiration from the sacrifice of Christ who espoused his Bride, the Church on the Cross.

Another aspect of the celebration of the sacraments is the

community. This is very evident in the new rites, and as such they envisage the active participation of the community. A fuller treatment and appreciation of the sacraments can be found in the ritual introductions to the new rites of the various sacraments, as well as in the rites themselves.

6) In the fifth Chapter of the *Constitution* we read: "Every week on the day which is called 'The Lord's Day' she keeps the memory of her Lord's resurrection." [11] It not only recalls the day of his triumph and the day when his work was crowned by the sending of the Holy Spirit, but it denotes a day consecrated to divine worship. There is a link between the Lord's Day and the Mass, the heart and centre of Catholic worship, bringing us into direct and life-giving contact with the Paschal Mystery. The Church has always regarded the Sunday as the weekly celebration of the Paschal Mystery. It is even more ancient than the festival of the Pasch. The *Constitution* says: "From that time (Pentecost) the Church has never failed to come together to celebrate the Paschal Mystery, celebrating the eucharist in which the victory and triumph of his death are made present." [12] We have accounts of such celebrations in the Acts of the Apostles and in the early writers: e.g., Ignatius, Justin and Tertullian. So intimately has every Sunday been associated with the Paschal Mystery that it has been called 'little Easter Sunday'.

From this very short survey of the Sunday celebration it is clear that it is intended to be the coming together of the community of the people of God to celebrate together the renewal of the Paschal Mystery. Active participation is a must. This demands constant instruction of the faithful so that it will in reality be a community celebration.

7) In his apostolic letter introducing the new Calendar (1969) Pope Paul wrote: "The influence of the Paschal

Mystery on each day, each week and the whole course of the year thereby shows us that the Paschal Mystery is at the heart of the whole Liturgical Year. This must be evident in the various seasons and in the feasts of the saints." Pius XII had already said in *Mediator Dei*: "The Liturgical Year is no cold lifeless representation of past events, no mere historical record. It is Christ himself, living on in his Church and still pursuing that path of boundless mercy. These mysteries are still now constantly present and active." [13] The *Constitution* is no less clear: "As each year passes by, she (the Church) unfolds the whole mystery of Christ from the Incarnation and birth until the Ascension, the day of Pentecost and the expectation of blessed hope and of the coming of the Lord. . . . The Church opens to the faithful the riches of her Lord's powers and merits, so that these are in some way made present for all time, and the faithful are enabled to lay hold upon them and become filled with saving grace." [14] The celebration of the Liturgical Year, which has as its apex the solemnity of the Pasch, has as the very centre of every feast, of every season, the eucharistic sacrifice. The very first feast, after that of Sunday, was the annual feast of the Pasch, the sacred Triduum. It is the most ancient season of the year and contains three dimensions. The first is a preparatory stage, that of Lent. This period developed as a time for repentance, a time too for preparation for baptism at the Paschal Vigil. In this period Christ is put before us (in the Lenten readings) as our Teacher. In the sacred Triduum itself we behold him as our high Priest, offering his sacrifice. The third stage is the Paschal Season, when the Spirit of the risen Christ dominates the scene.

Some three or four centuries later, Christmas, with its preparatory stage of Advent, and its prolongation until February 2nd was introduced. Other various feasts of Christ's life were introduced down the centuries. What we must always keep in mind is that each individual mystery, which is in reality an aspect of the one Mystery of Christ, is celebrated not in isolation but in relation to the whole mystery of redemption, the Paschal Mystery. This then gives the whole year a paschal outlook and a paschal meaning. The fact is that the whole Mystery of Christ, past, present and future is contained in each celebration. Every Mass contains the whole Mystery of Christ. Our capacity for grasping this is limited; we cannot grasp all at once the riches of the graces in the Mystery of Christ. We have as it were, to take this mystery apart, analyse its various aspects and thereby concentrate our attention on one aspect at a time thus becoming gradually permeated with the full meaning of the Mystery of Christ. Each feast, and each season, is thus built into the framework of the Paschal Mystery. The Incarnation and Birth of Christ, for example, were part of this Mystery. In every stage of his life, Christ merited grace for us as he lived each stage for us. This redemptive mission reached its summit on Calvary. He is still living his Paschal Mystery in all its aspects in his Church and in its members. "To accomplish so great a work, Christ is always present in his Church, especially in her liturgical actions" says the *Constitution*, and it adds: "the Liturgy is then rightly considered as an exercise of the priestly office of Christ and in this great work God is perfectly glorified and men are sanctified." (15) Thus the Liturgical Year brings us step by step to an ability to enter and participate in the Mystery of Christ.

Speaking of the Liturgical Year, the *Constitution* goes on to say: "In celebrating this annual cycle of Christ's Mysteries, Holy Church honours with especial love the Blessed Mary, Mother of God, who is inseparably involved in the saving work of her Son. In her the Church holds up and admires the most perfect fruit of the redemption." (16) This quotation makes it clear that none ever entered so fully into participation in the Paschal Mystery of Christ as did Mary his Mother. In his apostolic letter 'Marialis Cultus' of February 1974, Pope Paul VI develops this theme of Mary in the Liturgy. It is a wonderful exposition of Mary's place in the

Mystery of her Son and in the life of the Church. It will repay study. The third aspect of the Liturgical Year that the *Constitution* dwells on says: "The Church has also included in the annual cycle, days devoted to the memory of her martyrs and her saints. . . By celebrating the passage of these saints from earth to heaven the Church proclaims the Paschal Mystery achieved in those who have suffered and been glorified with Christ."(17) In those words the link between the Paschal Mystery and the saints is clear. We do not then regard them in isolation but as people who have participated in the Paschal Mystery of Christ, who lived it in their own lives from their baptism to the end and now share the glory of their Head.

8)   That thought brings us to the final point: that death is the final unfolding in all of us of the Paschal Mystery. It is a real sharing in Christ's own death, a sharing that leads to life eternal. The *Constitution* says on this subject: "The Rite for the burial of the dead should express more clearly the paschal character of Christian death." This has been beautifully enlarged on in the Introduction and in the new Rite itself. There we can read: "In the funeral rites the Church celebrates the Paschal Mystery of Christ. Those who in baptism have become one with the dead and risen Christ will pass with him from death to life and be welcomed into the fellowship of the saints in heaven. . . The Church therefore celebrates the eucharistic sacrifice of Christ's Passover for the dead." These thoughts linking death with Christ's Paschal Mystery find ample expression in the new Rite.

   The Liturgical Year draws to a close with a preview of the great finale in the celebration of the feast of Christ, the King. The final triumph of Christ when he comes again in glory to lead his elect into the Kingdom of his Father. That will be the completion of the working out of the Paschal Mystery in Christ's Mystical Body the Church. It will be the final chapter in the story of salvation-history, the story of the divine plan of love of the Triune God for us, a plan that centred around the Paschal Mystery, with its symbolic Pasch in the Old Testament, its realisation in Christ's redemptive work and its application to each succeeding generation through the Church's re-living in her Liturgy that Paschal Mystery. The foregoing section on the Paschal Mystery in the Liturgy is but a general survey. It will be treated in more detail in the second section of this book.

1. C.L. 5.
2. idem. 5.
3. idem. 10.
4. idem. 61.
5. idem. 7.
6. idem. 2.
7. idem. 102.
8. idem. 47.
9. idem. 59,61.
10. idem. 59,61.
11. idem. 102.
12. idem. 6.
13. M.D. 176.
14. C.L. 102.
15. idem. 7.
16. idem. 103.
17. idem. 104.

7. THE LITURGY OF THE SACRAMENTS

THE SACRAMENTS ARE FOR MAN

Christ has provided for the spiritual welfare of each succeeding generation through the Church he founded. The chief point of contact with Christ is in the liturgy, especially the liturgy of the sacraments. They are the specific means willed and instituted by Christ for rendering the fruits of his priesthood effective in the life of man. So the sacraments have their origin in the priestly sacrifice of Christ. Through the sacraments Christ takes our fundamental human situation and desires to raise it to a Christian situation. They are Christ entering into our lives to enable us to share in his paschal mystery. They aim at transforming us into the image of Christ and so sanctify almost every stage of our lives. The *Constitution on the Liturgy* deals with the sacraments in its third Chapter. There we read: "The purpose of the sacraments is to sanctify men, to build up the Body of Christ and finally to give worship to God; because they are signs they also instruct. They not only presuppose faith, but by words and objects they also nourish, strengthen and express it; that is why they are called 'sacraments of faith'. . . It is therefore of the highest importance that the faithful should easily understand the sacramental signs and should frequent with great eagerness those sacraments which were instituted to nourish the Christian life. . . The liturgy of the sacraments sanctifies almost every event in their lives; they are given access to the stream of divine grace which flows from the Paschal Mystery of the passion, death and resurrection of Christ, the font from which all the sacraments and sacramentals draw their power." (1)

THE SUPERNATURAL

Therefore in the liturgy of the sacraments, with its visible signs, the realities of the supernatural order become clear. We do not see life, only its outward manifestations; we do not hear a thought or see the soul of one who speaks to us; we only hear their words and see their actions.

In the sacraments we perceive the outward things (signs) but these tell us what Christ wishes to convey to us, namely, the invisible divine life of grace. A sacrament then is a visible sign, instituted by Christ to signify and to effect the sanctification it signifies. They are therefore not only signs of grace but also instruments of grace, powerful instruments in the hands of Christ for producing supernatural effects on the soul. Besides conferring sanctifying grace or increasing it (as in the case of the sacraments of the living) each sacrament has its own particular grace, conformable to the end for which it was instituted. This special grace is called sacramental grace. It gives the right to all those actual graces we need in view of the end for which each sacrament was instituted. Three of the sacraments, baptism, confirmation and holy orders, imprint what is called a character on the soul. This character is a special mark of relationship with the priesthood of Christ. It receives its name from the mark or stamp impressed on the bodies of those enrolled in the ancient imperial armies, expressing the idea of duty or service to one in public office. The sacrament of the eucharist is the centre of the whole sacramental system. That is why in the revision of the rites of each sacrament this link is stressed by its administration within the Mass, (except for the sacrament of penance though it too is closely linked).

THROUGH THE SENSES

It is through the senses man arrives at the knowledge of spiritual things. In the sacramental world we are greatly helped by the symbolism in which the liturgy abounds. To make this more apparent the *Constitution* tells us that the rites of the various sacraments are to be revised. This has now been completed. The new rites and prayers clearly indicate what takes place in the soul of man in the various stages of his supernatural life. Recalling such facts as birth, growth, renewal, fruitfulness, one becomes aware that these things are made spiritually real in the liturgy of the sacraments. It is instructive to note that it is through the body the soul is sanctified in each of the sacraments, thereby showing us that God wishes the sanctification of the whole man, body as well as soul. We must not look on the sacraments as something magical. This is clear from the fact, as the *Constitution* tells us, that the recipients must approach them with proper dispositions of soul, above all with faith, with unbounded confidence in the merits of Christ applied to the soul and with grateful love to our divine Benefactor. Through the sacraments we can keep in constant contact with Christ. Through them we are engrafted on to the Vine as living branches; through them we are strengthened, pruned and even restored to life. Through them we grow in Christ, who is our Head. As we study each sacrament we see Christ stand before us in a different role in each case, e.g., as our Brother, our King, our Physician, our Priest.

CELEBRATIONS

A point the *Constitution* draws our attention to is not the administration or reception of the sacraments but their celebration: "The very act of celebrating them effectively disposes the faithful to receive this grace fruitfully." [2] In other words they are liturgical celebrations and as such they are professions of faith. They are acts of worship. Another aspect of this celebration is the community aspect and as a result the Church's desire for active participation on the part of the faithful. This too is very evident in the new rites for the sacraments. The Christian people, as far as possible, should take part in them fully and actively.

Finally the *Constitution* tells us that the sacraments are sacraments of the Church and as such help in the building up of the Body of Christ, the Church. This ecclesiastical aspect brings home to us that the sacraments are not solely a personal relationship between Christ and the individual.

Right through them we can see that the sacramental system is closely bound up with Christ's redemptive work and now applied to the souls of men in and through the liturgy of these sacraments and thereby building up the Body of Christ, the Church.

---

1. C.L. 59, 61.
2. idem. 59.

8. LITURGY AND CHRISTIAN LIFE

The title indicates the practical application of the liturgy to our daily lives. The Council has stated that: "It is the primary and indispensable source of the true Christian spirit." [1] In other words, in and through the liturgy the Christian life will find a sure road to holiness of life, to union with God in Christ Jesus. It will teach the Christian programme, to die to sin and self, to live for God in Christ Jesus; "it will purify us, enlighten us, and unite us with Christ, the life of our souls."

Of the immense value of the liturgy for our Christian lives, St. Pius X declared: "If the faithful were well instructed in this matter and celebrated the feasts in the spirit that the Church willed in instituting them, a notable renewal and increase of faith, piety and religious instruction would be obtained and consequently the inner life of the faithful would thereby be reanimated and made better." [2] In *Mediator Dei* Pius XII wrote: "The sacred liturgy seeks to make the faithful share in the mysteries of Christ in such a way that the divine Head lives by his perfect holiness in each of his members." [3] The Vatican Council in its *Constitution on the Liturgy* reminds us that: "Although the liturgy is above all the worship of the divine Majesty, it nevertheless contains instruction for the faithful. For in the liturgy God speaks to his people and Christ is still proclaiming his gospel." [4]

We know the Mass is the greatest action of the liturgy and so its message and its graces should be the inspiration and support of the Christian people. Around the sacrificial altar the Christian soul learns the lesson of oblation of self in virtue of the example of Christ, who daily offers himself, an oblation, a sacrifice unto God. Since it is also our sacrifice, "we offer the immaculate victim not only through the hands of the priest but also with him, learn to offer ourselves through Christ, our Mediator; so that we be drawn day by day into ever more perfect union with God" (Constitution).(5) We know that the sacrifice is also life; we are fed with the bread of life, we are nourished at the table of the Lord's body which gives grace and strength to our souls here below and the promise of eternal life.

A very brief survey of the prayers and actions of the liturgy of the Mass will show how our Christian life can be renewed and strengthened by daily Mass. The penitential act awakens sentiments of humility and sorrow, a purifying of the soul in its approach to God. Similar sentiments are found in other parts of the Mass. Worthy indeed is God of praise, adoration, gratitude and so in a united voice we proclaim the majesty and greatness of the Triune God: "We praise Thee, we bless Thee, we glorify Thee, we give Thee thanks" (Gloria). The readings are a fresh promulgation of the Word of God. The Christ-Way of life is unfolded and we seem to hear the words of Saint Paul: "Let this mind be in you which is also in Christ Jesus" (Phil. 2:5). His teaching and example shine out and become a fresh challenge to follow him who has the words of life. Once more we hear the echo of the Father's message: "This is my beloved Son, hear ye him" (Matt. 17:5). He is for us the Way and the Truth. We must be prepared to be, not only "hearers of the word but doers also" as Saint James tells us.

At the Offertory we prepare to take part in the sacrifice. The gifts are brought to the altar. They are first of all God's gifts; bread and wine. They symbolise life for they sustain and nourish life. They also symbolise our own personal lives, for bread is the symbol of life's labour and wine the symbol of life's suffering. In offering those gifts to God we are offering ourselves, with our labours, our sufferings and our joys. These gifts represent ourselves all that we are and all that we have. They are in truth God's gifts for as Saint James says: "Every gift, every perfect gift is from above, coming down from our heavenly Father" (1:17). We do feel then the urge to thank him as our divine benefactor and we do so in the Preface. This prayer of thanks is in reality the opening words of the eucharistic prayer during which our gifts are changed into Jesus Christ. By the words of consecration the death and resurrection of Christ are enacted in a sacramental manner.

We are allowed to unite ourselves with our Redeemer in the offering of himself to the eternal Father and so priest and people "offer unto the most excellent majesty a pure host, a holy host, an immaculate host, the holy bread of life everlasting and the chalice of eternal salvation". At the end of the eucharistic prayer we can say with confidence: "Through him, with him, in him; in the unity of the Holy Spirit, all glory and honour is yours, almighty Father, for ever and ever."

The sentiments which filled the soul of Christ on the Cross should now be ours; sentiments of loving obedience and humble submission to his heavenly Father's Will. Since the Mass is the renewal of the new and eternal covenant, it should be the renewal of our covenant with God; a renewal of our pledge of love loyalty and obedience to our heavenly Father. It should be for us a fresh impetus to deny ourselves and bear our cross. It should inspire us to bring the spirit of our morning Mass to influence our daily Christian life. The sacrificial Banquet is the daily spiritual nourishment that strengthens the bond of love and union between Christ and the soul and the fellow-members of the Mystical Body of Christ.

The Postcommunion Prayers reveal the wonderful effects of this sacred banquet, and beg that those effects be brought about in our souls. Thus each day the liturgy of the Mass presents and communicates to souls the paschal mystery of Christ's death and resurrection. It can become the source of our daily spirit of self-giving and of our living for God in Christ Jesus. It will help to fulfil in us the words of Saint Paul: "The bearing about in our body the dying of Jesus, so that the life also of Jesus may be made manifest in our bodily frame" (2 Cor. 4:10-11).

Besides the daily liturgy of the Mass, the Church in her liturgical year offers us an annual path to holiness. *Mediator Dei* points out: "The liturgical year is no cold lifeless representation of past events, no mere historical record. It is Christ himself, living on in his Church, still pursuing that path of boundless mercy he began during his earthly life. This he did in order that souls might come into contact with his mysteries and, so to speak, live by them. And these mysteries are still constantly present and active." (6)

The *Constitution* adds: "As each year passes by she (the Church) unfolds the whole mystery of Christ from the incarnation and birth until the ascension, the day of Pentecost and the expectation of blessed hope and the coming of the Lord. Reflecting on these mysteries of redemption, the Church opens to the faithful the riches of her Lord's powers and merits and the faithful are enabled to lay hold upon them and become filled with saving grace." (7)

A brief look at it, as in the case of the Mass, will convince us of that truth. Accepting Advent as the start of another year of grace, we hear the Church's clarion call for a new beginning, her programme for the year ahead: "Put you on the Lord Jesus" (Rom. 13:14). The liturgy of Advent lays the foundation stone, humility in the realisation of the great need we have of Christ. We grasp that need from the scripture passages of the Old Testament, so frequent in Advent. The contemplation of his coming in the mystery of the incarnation is the highlight of Advent. To receive and welcome him when he comes to us now in grace will be a worthy preparation for his final and glorious coming at the end of time. Advent then should be a fresh awakening, a fresh start, a renewal of the spirit of our Christian vocation.

The Christmas-Epiphany liturgy is so sublime that the soul, who enters into the spirit of that season draws abundant instruction and grace from it. May we not sum it up in the words of that antiphon used at Christmas time: "O wonderful exchange etc."? The liturgy of Christmas-Epiphany stresses the fact of the new born babe in the manger as "He who was to come," the promised Saviour, the Prince of peace, the King, God's own Son. Viewed in the light of the Advent liturgy this season is certainly the climax and the fulfilment of the aspirations of Advent. Again are not the gifts of the Magi symbolic of the gifts Christ has brought?

Saint Ambrose says: "Open your treasures and offer him like gifts," namely, the gifts of our loyal, prayerful and self-sacrificing service. The Christmas period is all too short to assimilate its message. So in the weeks after Epiphany till February 2nd we go down to Nazareth and with Mary his Mother we keep these events in our hearts, pondering on them. The weeks spent in Nazareth remind us of the need for prayer in our lives. Beware of "the heresy of action", as Pius XII called it.

The Sundays of Lent tell of the need for penance, the motive that should inspire our spirit of penance, i.e., love and the fruits such a spirit begets. On the Sundays also, Christ appears before us as King, in conflict with our spiritual enemies, showing us how to react in similar circumstances. In those weekday Masses of Lent we listen to him as our Teacher, who instructs us with the words of life.

In the last week of Lent we behold him as our high Priest going forth to offer his sacrifice. The climax is reached with the celebration of the paschal mystery. The ancient rites for the catechumens and the penitents, as they prepared for baptism and reconciliation, still underline the liturgy of Lent, thereby making it a suitable preparation for the renewal at the paschal vigil.

The paschal mystery is the corner stone of the whole liturgical year. Christ's paschal mystery was enacted in us at baptism. That was our paschal mystery. It will find its completion in the eternal pasch, prefigured in the festival of the Ascension. The other paschal gift given us by Christ is the sacrament of penance. The paschal season closes with a fresh outpouring of the Holy Spirit at Pentecost. Intimately interconnected there are the sacraments of baptism, eucharist, penance, confirmation and holy orders. The paschal season is essentially the season of union. This is clear from the many passages in Christ's last discourse which are read after Easter.

The second half of the year of grace, perhaps less spectacular, is not lacking in its influence. The feasts of Corpus Christi and the Sacred Heart tell more of the eucharist and the love that inspired it. This Yearly Cycle continues dogmatic and moral teaching and aims at consolidating the progress already made. The observance of the Ember Days in each of the four Seasons of the year (no longer of obligation) offers days for spiritual renewal, a quarterly check-up. The doctrine of the Communion of Saints is underlined by the feasts of All Saints and All Souls. The yearly cycle closes with the feast of Christ the King. Also through the year, the lives of those souls who have faithfully followed Christ and now make part of the kingdom of the elect, are held up to our gaze. Apart from Mary, the Mother of Jesus and our Mother, they include the apostles and martyrs, the confessors and virgins, men and women from every race and station in life. All give an example and encouragement to follow them.

The *Constitution* expresses it thus: "In celebrating this annual cycle of Christ's mysteries, Holy Church honours with especial love the Blessed Mary, Mother of God, who is inseparably involved in the saving work of her Son. In her the Church holds up and admires the most perfect fruit of the redemption. . . The Church has also included in the annual cycle days devoted to the memory of her martyrs and her other saints. Raised up to perfection by the manifold grace of God, and already in possession of eternal salvation, they sing God's perfect praise in heaven and offer prayers for us. By celebrating the passage of these saints from earth to heaven the Church proclaims the paschal mystery achieved in those who have suffered and been glorified with Christ; she proposes them to the faithful as examples drawing all to the Father through Christ, and through their merits she pleads for God's favour. . . The feasts of the saints proclaim the wonderful works of Christ in his servants and display to the faithful fitting examples for their imitation." (8)

The closing Sundays of the year become, as it were, a preview of the final spiritual harvest, when the Christian soul will present the fruits of his life to the Master of the vineyard and in return will receive the reward promised to the faithful steward. The faithful soul will pass from the annual celebration of the liturgy to take part in the heavenly and eternal liturgy. "In the earthly liturgy we take part in a foretaste of the heavenly liturgy which is celebrated in the holy city of Jerusalem, toward which we journey as pilgrims." (9) *Mediator Dei* in its concluding lines prays that as we take part in the sacred liturgy during our earthly exile it may be a preparation and a prophetic token of the heavenly liturgy in which we shall one day participate.

Those who recite the divine office will find it an added help to enter into the spirit of the liturgical year. *Mediator Dei* says: "The ideal of the Christian life is the close and uninterrupted union of everyone with God. Therefore the worship which the Church pays to almighty God and which is founded mainly upon the eucharistic Sacrifice and the use of the sacraments, is so arranged that by means of the Divine Office it takes within its scope every hour of the day, every week, and the whole course of the year, all seasons and all the various phases of human life." [10] It is the prayer of the Mystical Body of Jesus Christ, offered to God in the name of all Christians and for their benefit.

The *Constitution* has this to say: "The Divine Office is devised so that the whole course of the day and night is made holy by the praises of God. It is truly the voice of the Bride addressed to her Bridegroom; it is the very prayer which Christ himself, together with his body, offers to the Father." [11]

Even from this short survey of the liturgical year we can see how true are the words of Pope St. Pius X: "For all without exception the greatest possible active and frequent participation in the liturgy is the normal and infallible path to solid piety." The Council also sees the liturgy as the means "for imparting an ever-increasing vigour to the Christian life," [12] which is the vital need of mankind at all times.

May we summarise these few pages on "the liturgy our life" in the words of Pope Pius XII: "It presents Christ to us, not only as an example to imitate, but as a teacher for us to believe, a shepherd for us to follow, as the advocate who saves, as the source of our holiness and as the mystical Head whose living members we are and whose life we live." [13] The *Constitution* notes: "From the liturgy, therefore, as from a font, grace is poured forth on us, and the sanctification of men in Christ and the glorification of God is achieved in the most efficacious possible way." [14]

---

1. C.L. 14.
2. Catechism of Christian Doctrine, Rome 1913.
3. M.D. 162.
4. C.L. 33.
5. idem. 48.
6. M.D. 176.
7. C.L. 102.
8. idem. 103, 104, 111.
9. idem. 8.
10. M.D. 146.
11. C.L. 84.
12. idem. 1.
13. M.D. 174.
14. C.L. 10.

Part II

THE

PASCHAL MYSTERY

IN OUR

CHRISTIAN LIFE

INTRODUCTION

The first part of this book dealt with a general survey of the Liturgy in the light of the *Constitution on the Sacred Liturgy*. Its objective was to indicate what the Liturgy is not, but especially to point out what it really is, and should mean to every individual who is striving to live a Christian Life. In such a general survey many points had to be treated, not in detail, but as part of the overall picture. Furthermore, as this book is primarily intended to help the ordinary faithful, it had to be presented in a simple manner. Its object is, as stated in the Introduction to the *Constitution*: "to impart an ever increasing vigour to the Christian Life of the faithful. . . whereby they may express in their lives and manifest to others, the 'Mystery of Christ'."[1]

Now in this second part, the aim envisaged is to show the practical application of the Liturgy to our Christian Life. It is inevitable that in this second part a certain amount of repetition will occur. This comes from the fact that it must be shown that the various parts of the Liturgy (studied in the first part) are not to be seen in isolation but as part of the whole Paschal Mystery, which is the very centre and core of the Liturgy. Through the Liturgy each generation can share in the graces won for us by Christ in his Paschal Mystery.

This second section of the book offers a way for each individual to get in contact with Christ, the life of the soul. That is why St. Pius X saw in the Liturgy "the indispensable source of the Christian Life". [2] The following pages aim at showing how to express in our own lives the 'Mystery of Christ' in and through the Liturgy. This will help us to enter into the very essence of the Liturgy, for it is life, supernatural life in Christ. It helps to form Christ in us so that he may live and reign in us. Pius XII in *Mediator Dei* has expressed all that in the words: "The sacred Liturgy seeks to make them (the faithful) share in such a way that the divine Head of the Mystical Body lives by his perfect holiness in each of his members. . . [3] It is Christ himself living on in his Church and still pursuing that path of boundless mercy which he began to tread during his life on earth. This he did in order that the souls of men might come into contact with his mysteries and, so to speak, live by them. These mysteries are still constantly present and active, excellent models of virtue for us to imitate, and also sources of divine grace for us because of the merits and intercession of the Redeemer. They live on in their effects in us." [4]

The *Constitution* sees the application of the Liturgy as: "The summit towards which all the activity of the Church is directed;" "The font from which all her powers flow;" [5] and as "an exercise of the priestly office of Jesus Christ", [6] whereby "the sanctification of man in Christ and the glorification of God is achieved in the most efficacious possible way." [7]

Such has been the teaching of the Popes, from St. Leo to Pope Paul VI as is clear from their words:

Pope St. Leo the Great: "The Liturgy is the sacrament of the Church."

Pope St. Gregory the Great: "The Liturgy is the pastoral foundation of the Life of the Church."

Pope St. Pius V: "The Liturgy is the sign of the unity of the Church."

Pope St. Pius X: "The Liturgy is the source of the true Christian spirit."

Pope Paul VI: "The Liturgy is the mystery of God's presence in this world, because the Liturgy makes us live off Christ, since the sacred liturgical signs bring us into the Kingdom of God."

1. C.L. 2.
2. idem. 14.
3. M.D. 162.
4. idem. 176.
5. C.L. 10.
6. idem. 7.
7. idem. 10.

1. THE PASCHAL MYSTERY
IN OUR CHRISTIAN LIFE

There are two passages in Sacred Scripture which underline the essential relationship between God and man: "God is love" (1 Jn. 4:8) and "I have loved thee with an everlasting love" (Jer. 31:3). The concrete expression of this love on the part of God is amply proved in the sending of his beloved Son to re-instate us as his children. The working out of this re-union of man with his God constitutes what we call salvation-history. It has a double aspect. The first is God's mission of love: "God so loved the world as to send his beloved Son that he might redeem those under the law" (the law of sin) (Gal. 4:4-5). This coming of the God-man involved on Christ's part a total surrender of himself to the Father's Will, to his plan "to restore all things in Christ" (Eph. 1:10). It is summed up by Saint Paul: "He humbled himself, taking the form of a servant, becoming obedient unto death, unto death on a cross, wherefore God hath exalted him" (Phil. 2:8). The Son of God paid the price of that surrender by offering his own life in sacrifice on the cross and returning to the Father through death, which led him to his glorious resurrection and ascension. That is what we call Christ's Paschal Mystery.

The Paschal Mystery of Christ was essentially a sacrifice, freely offered to the Father in obedience to his will. Jesus was in fact 'the suffering servant' spoken of by Isaias (53).

"Despised and the most abject of men, a man of sorrows and acquainted with infirmity. . . Surely he hath borne our infirmities and carried our sorrows; and we thought of him as it were a leper, and as one struck by God and afflicted. He was wounded for our iniquities, he was bruised for our sins. . . The Lord hath laid on him the iniquities of us all. He was offered because it was his own will. . . The Lord was pleased to bruise him in infirmity; if he shall lay down his life for sin he shall see a long-lived seed."

Christ's resurrection was the seal of the Father's approval on his sacrificial death, "Wherefore God hath exalted him" (Phil. 2:8). The Paschal Preface says the same thing: "By dying he destroyed our death and by rising he restored our life."

Saint John places his description of the Passion within the framework of the Paschal Mystery: "Jesus, knowing that his hour was come that he should pass out of this world to the Father, having loved his own who were in the world, he loved them unto the end (Jn. 13:1). . . These things were done that the scripture be fulfilled: 'You shall not break a bone of him' " (Jn. 19:36).

Even during his life we see Christ himself portray his divine mission, "to seek that which was lost," in such parables as the good shepherd, the lost sheep, the father and his prodigal son. He uses such phrases as: "lost and was found," "dead and come to life," "laying down his life and taking it up again." In the early Church we find symbols conveying the same idea: we see in the catacombs, paintings of the shepherd carrying the lost sheep (just found) on his shoulder, the cross with the paschal lamb on it, the cross with the Christ in glory upon it.

The second aspect of the Paschal Mystery in salvation-history centres on man. He is expected to make a response to God's love. God wishes man to accept willingly the treaty signed in the blood of his Son. The risen Christ, especially through the liturgy of the mass and the sacraments, continues to be our Saviour and Redeemer, applying to us the merits and fruits of his Paschal Mystery; "Of his fulness we have all received, grace for grace" (Jn. 1:16); "He continues for ever, he has an everlasting priesthood whereby he is able to save them that come to God through him, ever living to make intercession for us" (Heb. 7:24-25). That fulness of divine life was first communicated by the eternal Word of God to the humanity of Christ at the moment of the incarnation and is now imparted to us by Christ. His humanity has become the instrument of our salvation, our reconciliation with the Father. So Christ's Paschal Mystery is still active and present. It becomes our paschal mystery, making us pass from death (the death of sin and slavery) to a sharing in the divine life here below and later in glory with Christ. We become heirs, joint heirs with Christ. This is clearly outlined for us in the opening paragraph of the *Constitution on the Sacred Liturgy* of Vatican II. "God who wills that all men be saved, sent his Son, the Word made flesh. . . he achieved his task principally by the Paschal Mystery of his blessed passion, resurrection from the dead and glorious ascension, whereby 'dying he destroyed our death and rising he restored our life'. Just as Christ was sent by the Father, so also he sent the apostles. . . that they might proclaim that the Son of God, by his death and resurrection had freed us from the power of Satan and from death and brought us into the kingdom of his Father. His purpose also was that they might accomplish the work of salvation, which they had proclaimed, by means of sacrifice and sacraments, around which the entire liturgical life revolves." [1] So in their preaching, as recorded in their writings, we find they always show the unity between passion and resurrection, redemption and sanctification. Saint Peter in his first letter writes: "You were not redeemed with corruptible things, as silver or gold. . . but with the precious Blood of Christ, as of a Lamb unspotted. . . God raised him from the dead and has given him glory" (Pet. 1:18-21). Saint Paul, without using the term 'Paschal Mystery', clearly states what it is: "The mystery hidden from eternity. . . to restore all things in Christ" (Eph. 1:9). "Christ died for all that they also may not live to themselves but unto him who died for them and rose again" (2 Cor. 5:15). "That I may know him and the power of his resurrection and the fellowship of his sufferings, being made conformable to his death" (Phil. 3:10). "Buried with him in baptism, in whom you are risen again" (Col. 2:12). "If you are risen with him, seek the things that are above" (Col. 3:1).

Since the liturgy is set within the framework of salvation-history, it gives prominence to the Paschal Mystery. The great mission of the Church is the building up of the Body of Christ. The Church is paschal in its origin for the *Constitution* says: "It was from the side of Christ upon the cross there came forth the wondrous sacrament of the whole Church."[2] It is paschal in its programme and so the Paschal Mystery must play an important role in the apostolate, especially in the liturgy, whether it be the liturgy of the word or the sacramental liturgy. This too is stated in the *Constitution*: "The liturgy is the summit towards which the activity of the Church is directed; at the same time it is the font from which all her power flows[3] . . . For members of the faithful the liturgy of the sacraments and sacramentals sanctifies every event of life; they are given access to the stream of divine grace which flows from the Paschal Mystery of the Passion, death and resurrection of Christ, the font from which they draw their power."[4] A subsequent instruction affirms the absolute predominance of the Paschal Mystery in Christian living. Christians therefore can and

must express the Paschal Mystery of Christ in their own lives, for it is the very heart of the Christian life. Its whole object is, as Saint Paul says: "that they may live no longer for themselves but for him who died for them and rose again" (2 Cor. 5:15). The heart and soul of salvation-history is Christ's Paschal Mystery and so it must be the heart and soul of Christianity as the expression of man's response to God's love for him. Through the liturgy then Christians throughout the ages can overcome time and space and come into contact with the living, risen Christ, "Who is yesterday, today and the same for ever" (Heb. 13:8). The Church, the Body of Christ, is therefore living out in each successive generation the reality of the Paschal Mystery "until he comes".

A more detailed study of the *Constitution on the Sacred Liturgy* will show the all-important place and role that the Paschal Mystery of Christ must hold in our Christian life. It is mentioned in four of the seven chapters of the *Constitution*. That all this is so can also be seen from the gospel. There we learn that Christ lived his mystery (in its various aspects) for us: "I came that they may have life" (Jn. 10:10). Throughout his life he offered himself as a model: "I am the way" (Jn. 14:6). "Come, follow me" (Matt. 9:9). "No man cometh to the Father but by me" (Jn. 14:6). We can likewise claim the mystery of Christ as ours because the Father willed to make us his children, to make us holy in Christ. "He chose us in Christ that we should be holy" (Eph. 1:4). It is the liturgy that puts us in contact with Christ who is our way and our life. That is why the *Constitution* says: "The liturgy is the exercise of the priestly office of Jesus Christ. . . In the liturgy the sanctification of man is effected [5]. . . Although the sacred liturgy is above all things worship of the divine majesty, it nevertheless contains much instruction for the faithful [6]. . . from the liturgy the sanctification of men in Christ and the glorification of God is achieved in the most efficacious possible way [7]. . . The liturgy is the outstanding means whereby the faithful may express in their lives and manifest to others the mystery of Christ and the real and true nature of the Church." [8] To appreciate the meaning and value of the liturgy as the means of getting in contact with the Paschal Mystery and participating in it, the *Constitution* encourages both education and instruction so that "full and active participation by all the faithful is the aim to be considered, for it is the primary and indispensable source from which they are to derive the true Christian spirit. . . This is their right and duty by reason of their baptism." [9] Later on it adds: "This is a sign of the providential dispositions of God in our time, as a movement of the Holy Spirit in his Church. It is today a distinguishing mark of the Church's life." [10] A clear knowledge of the meaning and the depth of the Paschal Mystery is essential if we are to live our supernatural lives to the full, if we are to live out that mystery in our own lives, day by day and year by year. That is what St. Paul had in mind when he said: "For me to live is Christ" (Phil. 1:21). "I live, now not I, but Christ lives in me" (Gal. 2:20). "I labour among you that Christ be formed in you" (Gal. 4:19). Right through life from the moment a person begins his transitus from the baptismal font to his final transitus at death, his whole life is one of death and resurrection, a dying to sin and self so that Christ may live and reign in him. The *Constitution* sees in such a life, which participates in the Paschal Mystery through the liturgy, a foretaste of that heavenly liturgy celebrated in the celestial Jerusalem. A fundamental approach to the Paschal Mystery must be one of faith; a real living faith in Christ. It is not just mere acceptance of a truth but a living faith in all that the God-man, Jesus Christ, really means. He is not a mere historical figure we read about in the New Testament, but a person, a divine person, still living, still active, in our very midst by means of his priesthood. The *Constitution* says: "Christ is always present in his Church, especially in her liturgical actions. . . The Liturgy is considered as an exercise of the priestly office of Jesus Christ." [11] It is faith that reveals to us the wonders of the Paschal Mystery not only in Christ himself but also in us.

There may be a danger that we isolate our Christian Life from its very source, the Paschal Mystery. We may, as it were, divide it into compartments. The very first Chapter of the *Constitution* shows us that the Paschal Mystery was the foundation-stone of the Christian Life for the early Christians, it was their path of holiness. The *Constitution on the Church* reminds us that all the people of God are called to holiness of life, and adds that the same holiness is fostered by all. This holiness is a sharing in the holiness of Christ. No doubt clergy and religious, as the various Council Documents point out, are called to a more intimate, sharing in the Paschal Mystery. But for all the Christian Life is one in essence, one in its object, the unfolding and the developing to the full in each soul the mystery of Christ, his Paschal Mystery, initiated in each one at baptism. Pope Paul VI says: "The Paschal Mystery is also the mystery of salvation."

To have a full picture of this 'mystery of Christ' as St. Paul calls it, one must view it in its three fold dimension; its foreshadowing in the Old Testament, its reality in Christ in the New Testament, and its prolongation in the Church through the liturgy. In living the Paschal Mystery the Church has gradually formed her liturgical year, each feast and each season having the Paschal Mystery as its centre. So Pius XII in *Mediator Dei* writes: "In obedience to her Founder's wishes the Church prolongs the priestly mission of Jesus Christ, mainly through the sacred liturgy." (12) She does this through the renewal of his sacrifice in the Mass, by means of the sacraments, and in the course of the liturgical year. The *Constitution* draws our attention to an important prerequisite if the liturgy is to be able to produce its full effects; it is necessary that the faithful come to it with proper dispositions, that they cooperate with divine grace lest they receive it in vain. [13] It prays that the liturgy will move the faithful to be 'one in holiness' and that "they may hold fast in their lives to what they have grasped by their faith." [14]

1. C.L. 5, 6.
2. idem. 5.
3. idem. 10.
4. idem. 61.
5. idem. 7.
6. idem. 33.
7. idem. 10.
8. idem. 2.
9. idem. 14.
10. idem. 43.
11. idem. 7.
12. M.D. 2.
13. C.L. 11.
14. idem. 10.

2. THE PASCHAL MYSTERY IN THE OLD TESTAMENT

The *Constitution on the Sacred Liturgy* in its very opening paragraph states: "The wonderful works of God among the people of the Old Testament were but a prelude to the work of Christ, the Lord, in redeeming mankind." [1] The letter to the Hebrews says: "God in divers manners spoke in times past to the fathers by the prophets, last of all in these days hath spoken to us by his Son" (Heb. 1:1-2). To see the divine plan unfolding itself one must go back and see "the wonderful works of God". We may regard the very first hint of God's intervention to rectify the damage done by the fall of our first parents was when driving them forth from the garden. He then promised that a time would come when he would put enmities between the serpent (the devil) and a woman and her seed and the latter would be victorious. For centuries God willed to prepare man for the great revelation of the mystery of Christ. He waited so long because man, as the result of the fall, was incapable and unworthy of such a manifestation. He had fallen because of pride and disobedience and so only after long experience of his weakness and misery would he realise the need he had of a Saviour.

In the light of the New Testament we now see more clearly that some of the wonderful works of God were a foreshadowing of this future liberation e.g., the deluge, the call of Abraham, and the command to sacrifice his only son,

Isaac. The most outstanding of the wonderful works was the liberation of the future chosen people from the slavery of Egypt, under the leadership of Moses. We are familiar today with the many efforts of liberating enslaved peoples and giving them the gift of freedom. The great liberation in the Old Testament was the Exodus. It led to the birth of a new people, a chosen people, the people of God, a holy nation. Another such liberation of these same people was to take place centuries later, after their captivity in Babylon. The events of their first liberation are described for us in the Book of Exodus. God himself prescribed the manner and details of this liberation; the sacrifice and eating of the lamb, the sprinkling of their door posts with its blood, the passage of the destroying angel, who slew the first born of man and beast, the saving of all those whose door posts were signed with the blood of the lamb, their sudden departure on that night from Egypt, the crossing of the Red Sea in safety, while their pursuing enemies were drowned. After two months journeying they came to Sinai. There God concluded a covenant with them, whereby they became his people. That covenant was ratified in blood, the blood of the sacrifice offered by Moses. This triple event, the sacrifice of the lamb, the liberation from Egypt and the covenant at Sinai, which make up the full story of the Exodus, are no doubt clear symbols of the Paschal Mystery of Christ and eventually of our sharing in it. The Paschal Mystery of Christ is in reality another liberation, that of mankind from the slavery of sin and Satan. In the story of Exodus we have not only the symbol of Christ's Paschal Mystery but that of his followers, through the sacrament of baptism. As the chosen people of old made their journey to the land of promise, we find other wonderful works of God done on their behalf; such as feeding them in the desert with the miraculous Manna and giving them drink from the rock, the destruction of enemies they encountered on their journey. So important was the Exodus that God commanded his people to celebrate it each year in a twofold festival; one recalling the events of the actual exodus and the other the events at Sinai. The former became the festival of the Pasch, the latter that of Pentecost. This twofold celebration was more than a mere recalling of historical events. It was a re-living, a renewal of the spirit which animated their fore-fathers. The Jewish Ritual even today has those words: "It is not our ancestors only that the Most Holy redeemed from Egypt but us also did he redeem with them." There were other renewals during the course of their history e.g., after the Babylonian captivity, under the priest Esdras. We also have their prayerful reflections on the Exodus in the psalms, especially psalms 77 and 135.

But the chosen people were not always loyal to their God and their covenant with him. They often rebelled, they fell into idolatry. God had to punish them time and again. Yet God, through all these centuries, welcomed them back to his friendship when they repented. He spoke to them through his prophets. He spoke of repentance, of renewal, of hope in a future Messiah. Messianic prophecies were delivered by the prophets: they foretold many details of his coming, his mission, of the new covenant and the new pasch he would inaugurate. The prophets foresaw him as the suffering servant of God, one who would bear their sins, be wounded for their iniquities. He would be the true paschal lamb. They also pictured him as the new Moses, the new David who would establish a new kingdom and rule with justice, love and mercy. Pen-pictures of the Messiah are so detailed that they should recognise him when he would come. He will be descended from the royal house of David, be born in the city of David, Bethlehem, his mother will be a virgin. He will in all truth be 'Emmanuel', 'God with us.' Not only the prophecies but the prophets themselves were in certain ways figures of the Messiah; e.g., Moses, David, Jeremiah, Daniel. The letter to the Hebrews outlines the priesthood of the Old Law as a symbol, if as yet imperfect, of the priesthood of the Messiah. It refers too to the annual paschal sacrifice as but a figure of the new pasch. At first sight it seems difficult to reconcile the characteristics the prophets give to the future Messiah. Some of these traits belong to God alone, he is to be a king and yet the suffering servant.

For many people the Old Testament is a closed book. It was not always so. The early Fathers of the Church clearly showed the value of the Old Testament for us. Saint Augustine, for example, says: "In the Old Testament the New Testament is hidden and in the New Testament the Old appears." How true that is when we recall the words of Christ himself: "You study the Scriptures, believing that in them you have eternal life; now these same Scriptures testify to me" (Jn. 5:39). After his resurrection when conversing with the two disciples on the road to Emmaus, "Beginning at Moses and all the prophets he expounded to them in all the Scriptures the things that were concerning him" (Lk. 24:27). They were afterwards to say to one another, "were not our hearts burning within us while he spoke and opened to us the Scriptures?" (Lk. 24:32).

What we must not overlook is the fact that the Old Testament is also the Word of God. It is God revealing himself to his chosen people. It is part of salvation-history. Neither must we forget that Jesus himself was trained in the tradition of the Old Testament. He heard it read and explained each Sabbath in the Synagogue. His prayer-life was nourished with the psalms of the Old Testament. When Christ began his preaching he utilised the Old Testament to explain his mission and to show that he himself was the long-expected Messiah. Many of his parables have their counter-part in the Old Testament, e.g., the Vineyard which bore no fruit, the Vineyard the owner let out on hire (Matt. 21).

This same approach was to be used by the apostles and the evangelists. The gospel of St. Matthew is full of references to the Old Testament. He frequently puts on the lips of Jesus the words: "That the Scriptures might be fulfilled."

Saint Matthew's gospel is often called "the gospel of fulfilment'. Saint Paul speaks of the Exodus and the journey through the desert and remarks, "with many of them God was not well pleased" (1. Cor. 10:5). Again he told the Romans that all those things that had been written were written for our instruction (Rom. 15:4). Apart from their Jewish upbringing, the apostles understood that God had not two distinct messages. It was the same God who spoke through the prophets of old and who acted through the events of the history of the chosen people. All the time he was preparing for the coming of his Word made flesh. When we read the New Testament we must do so in the light of the Old. It is interesting to note how the *Constitution on the Church* refers to the close link between the Old and New Testaments. "Already from the beginning of the world the foreshadowing of the Church took place. She was prepared for in a remarkable way throughout the history of the people of Israel and by means of the ancient Covenant." (2) Just as Christ was the fulfilment in his person and work of the Old Testament, so the Church sees herself as the new people of God, the new Jerusalem, the new Kingdom of God. In describing her the *Constitution* uses many images from the Old Testament. The Dogmatic Constitution on Divine Revelation mentions the value and link between the Old Testament and the New. In the Decree on Non-Christian Religions we find a clear statement on the spiritual bond linking the people of the new Covenant with Abraham's stock. This is referred to in the 11th chapter of the letter to the Hebrews. The *Constitution on the Sacred Liturgy* leaves us in no doubt about the value of the Old Testament when it speaks about Sacred Scripture and its use in the liturgy. Liturgical piety is essentially scriptural. One has only to look through the various liturgical books to realise this. The *Constitution* says: "Sacred Scripture is of the greatest importance in the celebration of the liturgy (3). . . The treasures of the bible are to be opened up more lavishly, so that richer fare may be provided for the faithful at the table of God's word [4]. . . He is present in his word, since it is he himself who speaks when Holy Scriptures are read in Church [5]. . . In the liturgy God speaks to his people and Christ is still proclaiming his gospel." [6] That is why it could also say: "From that time onward (1st Pentecost) the Church has never failed to come together to celebrate the Paschal Mystery; reading those things which were in all the scriptures concerning him." [7]

We can glean from the writings of the early Fathers, from the rites used in the liturgy of the sacraments, and from the paintings in the catacombs, how the symbols used from the Old Testament found their reality in the New. They had an educational value for those early Christians and so they should also have value for us. The liturgy today has increased the amount of reading from the Old Testament. Each Sunday (outside the Paschal Time) has one reading from the Old Testament and usually it has its counterpart in the gospel of that day. The first reading on the week-days of Lent (as of old) is always from the Old Testament. Then on week-days during the Yearly Cycle the first reading is from the Old Testament every second year. That is our interest in the Old Testament. It shows us God's wonderful works among his chosen people. It constitutes the initial chapters in the story of salvation-history. It is the divine preparation for the great exodus, the Paschal Mystery of Christ and his followers in the New Testament. It brings home to us the unchangeable love of God for us and once more should evoke in us the response he expected from the chosen people of old. We can apply to ourselves the words of Saint Paul to the Romans: "Whatsoever was written was for our instruction" (Rom. 15:4).

---

1. C.L. 5.
2. C.Ch. 2.
3. C.L. 24.
4. idem. 51.
5. idem. 7.
6. idem. 33.
7 idem. 6.

3. THE PASCHAL MYSTERY IN THE NEW TESTAMENT

The *Constitution on the Sacred Liturgy* in its first Chapter says: "He (Christ) achieved his task principally by the Paschal Mystery of his blessed passion, resurrection from the dead and glorious ascension, whereby 'dying he destroyed our death and rising he restored our life."(1) The chosen people, as we saw, were liberated and set free by the blood of the paschal lamb. Our Saviour is the true paschal lamb. The paschal lamb of the Jews did not conquer sin and death by rising again but Christ did both. He was crucified, died and was buried and the third day he rose from the dead. Christ, in foretelling his passion and death, always linked them with his resurrection. Passion, death and resurrection constitute Christ's own Paschal Mystery. "Behold, we go up to Jerusalem; and all things shall be accomplished which were written by the prophets concerning the Son of Man. For he shall be delivered to the Gentiles and shall be mocked and scourged and spat upon. And after they have scourged him, they will put him to death. And the third day he shall rise again" (Lk. 18:31-32). Not only did he link them together but his Paschal Mystery was ever before him as is clear from the gospel story. In his youth he went to the temple for the Jewish feast of the Pasch. When he was about to begin his public ministry he went to be baptised by John the Baptist. The latter pointed him out as "The Lamb of God who would take away the sins of the world" (Jn. 1:29). In verse 35-36 Saint John again notes: "The next day John stood and two of his disciples, and beholding Jesus walking, he said: Behold the Lamb of God." Here it may be of interest to pause and recall the place the lamb finds in the Scriptures. It is strange that ever since the advent of sin man has had need of the lamb. Abel drew down upon himself the blessing of God by the offering of a lamb. Abraham went to the mountain, at the command of God, to offer in sacrifice his only son, Isaac, and found there a ram caught by the horns to offer instead. To Moses God decreed the offering of the paschal lamb and the shedding of its blood as a protection against the destroying angel. Isaiah prayed that "the lamb, the ruler of the earth be sent" (Is. 16:1). He also saw in a vision that ruler led as a lamb to the slaughter (Is. 53).

Describing for us the beauty of heaven, Saint John in the Apocalypse tells us: "The Lamb is the lamb thereof" (Apoc. 21:23). He also saw the Lamb on the throne surrounded by a multitude whom no man could number, of every nation and tribe and people and tongue, clothed with white robes and palms in their hands and they sang a new canticle: The Lamb that was slain is worthy to receive power and divinity, and honour and glory and benediction" (Apoc. 5:12). He heard a voice saying: "These are they. . . who have washed their robes in the blood of the Lamb (Apoc. 7:14). Speaking again of heaven Saint John says: "Blessed are they who are called to the marriage supper of the Lamb" (Apoc. 19:9). So for the chosen people and for the infant Church the lamb was a sacred symbol.

On the occasion of his visit to the temple for the feast of the Pasch, in the first year of his public life, Christ drove out of the temple those who would desecrate it, his Father's House. On that occasion he referred to the temple of his own body, its destruction and its resurrection: "Destroy this temple and in three days I will build it up again" (Jn. 2:19-

103

23). Other incidents occur in the gospel which show that Christ always had in mind his Paschal Mystery. How often he speaks of it as "His Hour" and of the freedom with which he would go forth to his passion and death. "I lay down my life that I may take it up again" (Jn. 10:18). The parable of the good shepherd laying down his life for his sheep is a figure of himself. When the end drew near he sent two disciples to prepare to celebrate the Pasch: "I have desired to celebrate this Pasch with you before I suffer" (Lk. 22:15); "After I shall have risen, I will go before you into Galilee" (Matt. 26:32). It was at this paschal feast that he inaugurated the Pasch of the new Covenant, which would renew for all time his own Paschal Mystery. Saint John, in his account of the passion of Christ, gives greater emphasis to the paschal character of Christ's death. He was sacrificed at the time the lambs were being immolated in the temple. He compared Christ to the paschal lamb; "Not a bone of his would be broken" (as prescribed for the paschal lamb) (Jn. 19:36). He also makes clear the link between the Jewish Pasch and that of Christ: "Before the festival day of the Pasch, Jesus knowing that his hour had come that he should pass out of this world to the Father (Jn. 13:1); "I came forth from the Father and am come into the world, again I leave the world and I go to the Father" (Jn. 16:28). Here Christ states clearly the two aspects of his Paschal Mystery. At the end of the Paschal Supper he arose and said: "Arise, let us go" (Jn. 14:31). Where? He went forth to the garden to begin his sorrowful passion that was to lead to Calvary, where he was crucified, died and was buried. The details are outlined for us in the gospels. We are familiar with them. Is it not all summed up for us by Christ himself in the words: "Greater love than this no man hath than to lay down his life for his friends" (Jn. 15:13). Saint Peter, speaking of the passion, sees it in terms of the lamb: "You were redeemed not with corruptible things, as gold or silver, but with the precious blood of Christ, as of a lamb, unspotted and undefiled"

(1 Pt. 1:18-19). Saint Paul gives us his thoughts on the Paschal Mystery: "Christ our Pasch is sacrificed" (1 Cor. 5:7); "When we were enemies we were reconciled to God by the death of his Son" (Rm. 5:10). "He delivered himself for me, a sacrifice, an oblation unto God" (Eph. 5:2). "In whom we have redemption through his blood, the remission of sins" (Col. 13:14); "Blotting out the handwriting of the decree against us fastening it to the cross" (Col. 2:14). Saint Paul does not finish at the cross, he too joins it with the resurrection: "From a man came death and by a man the resurrection" (1 Cor. 15:21). He sees Christ as the new Adam, the new Moses, leading his people from slavery to freedom. The 15th Chapter of his first letter to the Corinthians is all on the doctrine of Christ's resurrection and ours. Christ's Paschal Mystery was completed only on the day of his resurrection and his enthronement at his ascension. The greatest events in salvation-history, even the greatest moments of human achievements pale away before the fact of Christ's resurrection. That was the turning point in the history of man. But the risen Christ can only be known by faith. It is his Spirit that enables us to believe. Truly did Christ say: "I am the resurrection and the life" (Jn. 11:25). Saint Paul was absolutely convinced of Christ's resurrection, for he said: "If Christ be not risen from the dead, our preaching is in vain" (1 Cor. 15:14); "If there be no resurrection, then Christ is not risen; Christ is risen from the dead, the first fruits of those who sleep" (1 Cor. 15:20). After his resurrection, when conversing with the two disciples on the road to Emmaus, Christ once more linked his passion and resurrection: "Ought not Christ have suffered those things and so enter into his glory" (Lk. 24:26).

The Paschal Mystery is the mystery Saint Paul speaks about in his letter to the Ephesians: a mystery hidden in God but now revealed in all its fulness in the death and resurrection of Christ. It is the mystery of the divine plan of man's redemption, of man's reunion with his God. It is the

105

mystery of divine love and mercy in action, the mystery prepared for in the earlier stages of salvation-history in the Old Testament and now revealed in all its splendour in the New Testament. This mystery grows still more wonderful when we realise that it is renewed in every Mass. The Liturgical Year relives it in its historical details, thus making present the saving actions of Christ, bringing into the living present the reality of his salvific and Paschal Mystery. This is what the *Constitution* has in mind when in its first chapter it says: "Just as Christ was sent by the Father, so also he sent the apostles. . . This he did that, by preaching the gospel to every creature, they might proclaim that the Son of God, by his death and resurrection, had freed us from the power of Satan and from death, and brought us into the kingdom of his Father. His purpose also was that they might accomplish the work of salvation, which they had proclaimed, by means of sacrifice and sacraments, around which the entire liturgical life revolves." [2]

The Paschal Mystery also teaches us the meaning and solution of the problem of human suffering. The cross is the symbol of human suffering and the suffering Saviour who died on that cross and rose from the dead is the solution. Saint Paul tells us he gloried in his sufferings in order to become conformable to Christ, Christ crucified. He says: "If we suffer with Christ, we shall reign with him and the sufferings of this time are momentary and light in comparison with the reward to come" (Rm. 17:18). Here again he joins the two aspects of the Paschal Mystery, suffering and glory. We make the same thought our own in the prayer we say so often: "May we, by his passion and death be brought to the glory of the resurrection."

It is not without interest to note that the gospel of the Transfiguration is read on the second Sunday of Lent. Moses and Elias came and conversed with Jesus about his exodus, his passion and death; thus linking Thabor and Calvary. Thabor is the symbol of the victory of Calvary and so is an encouragement to us in our following of Christ. Through our sharing in the Paschal Mystery in baptism, we too set out on the road to Jerusalem, the heavenly one. This demands that we face up to the difficulties we meet on the way. Like Abraham of old, we set out with faith and confidence, knowing the victory will be ours. We must pass over the Mount of Calvary like Christ, but like him too it will lead to the Mount Thabor, the symbol of final victory and triumph. It is in our day-to-day living of our Christian lives, with its ups and downs, that we are sharing in his sufferings, reproducing the pattern of his death, and this process will one day lead us to share in his resurrection. That is what Saint Paul has in mind when he writes: "That I may know him and the power of his resurrection and the fellowship of his sufferings, being made conformable to his death. If by any means I may attain to the resurrection. . . Not that I had already attained or were already perfect. . . I press forward towards the mark, the prize of the supernal **vocation of God in Christ Jesus" (Ph. 10:14). Saint Paul is** showing us in his own case the reality and the unfolding of the Mystery of Christ, the Paschal Mystery, a mystery of death and life. He sees Christ as the source, the strength and the model. That is what he says elsewhere: "For me to live is Christ" (Ph. 1:21).

---

1. C.L. 5.
2. idem. 6.

4. THE PASCHAL MYSTERY AND THE EUCHARIST

The second chapter of the *Constitution on the Sacred Liturgy* deals exclusively with the Holy Eucharist. On the night before he suffered Christ instituted, within the framework of the Jewish Paschal Festival, the renewal of his own Paschal Mystery. The *Constitution* expresses it thus: "At the Last Supper, on the night he was betrayed, our Saviour instituted the eucharistic sacrifice of his body and blood. . . He did this in order to perpetuate the sacrifice of the Cross throughout the centuries until he should come again; he wished to entrust to his beloved Spouse, the Church, a memorial of his death and resurrection, a sacrament of love. . . a paschal banquet." [1] In the Mass then we have the fountain from which flows all our liturgy. The Church is now the new people of God, and the Mass is the covenant-sacrifice of the New Law. It is the Christian Pasch.

This has been the teaching of the Church from earliest times, confirmed by the Council of Trent, which says: "Christ instituted the New Pasch, in which he is immolated under the appearances of visible signs (bread and wine) in memory of his passing to the Father." The Hebrew paschal rite prolonged in time the Exodus (their liberation and election as the people of God). Likewise Christ sees his death (a sacrificial one) as the liberation of mankind from the slavery of sin and their call to be the new people of God, sharing in his risen life. Just as the Jewish Passover in the Exodus was changed from an historical event to a paschal rite, ordained by God, so Christ instituted a paschal rite to recall and renew his own Passover, his Pasch. In instituting this new rite Christ did so within the framework of the Jewish paschal rite. In the Jewish historical Pasch (the Exodus) we find three essential elements; the word of God, the immolation of the lamb, and the supper of the lamb. In the ritual paschal rite of the Jews the same elements are found; the word of God in the explanation of the rite and the chanting of psalms, and the partaking of the lamb, earlier immolated in the temple. Christ, following this pattern, proclaimed the New Law in his last discourse, offered the bread and wine, now changed into his body and blood (to be later immolated on the Cross) to his apostles: "Take and eat, this is my body which shall be given for you; drink ye all of this, this is my blood which shall be shed for you." That he wished them to renew this paschal rite is clear from his command, "Do this in memory of me; as often as you do these things you shall show forth the death of the Lord until he comes." Such then is the manner of renewal of Christ's Paschal Mystery (death-resurrection). That is the parting gift to his Church. It has now become the Church's sacrifice, the one and only sacrifice of the New Law, identical with his own historical sacrifice on Calvary. It is the heritage handed on to us in the Mass. The Mass also follows the same pattern. After the introductory rite, there is the liturgy of the word, the promulgation of God's Law. In the eucharistic liturgy the offering of the sacrifice of the New Law is accomplished within the Eucharistic Prayer. The sacred banquet of the immaculate lamb is in the communion rite. The *Constitution* points out this triple aspect: "The treasures of the bible are to be opened up more lavishly, so that richer fare may be provided for the faithful at the table of God's word [2]. . . God speaks to his people and Christ is still proclaiming his gospel [3]. . . They should be instructed by

God's word and be nourished at the table of the Lord's body. . . by offering the immaculate victim not only through the hands of the priest, but also with him, they should learn to offer themselves through Christ their Mediator; they should be drawn day by day into ever more perfect union with God and each other." [4]

The very centre and heart of the Mass is the Eucharistic Prayer, extending from the Preface to the Our Father, exclusive. Everything else in the Mass leads up to the Eucharistic Prayer or flows from it. It is within that prayer that the sacrifice is enacted. To understand and appreciate the reality enshrined within the Eucharistic Prayer it is necessary to go back to the Jewish Paschal Supper. The evangelists tell us: "He gave thanks." They do not give us the words of thanks used by Christ. No doubt they were the words used and prescribed in their ritual. "To give thanks" (Beracoth in Hebrew, Eucharistia in Greek) meant both praise and thanksgiving. It was a prayer of praise, blessing and gratitude to God for his wonderful works, not merely his creative deeds but also his special revelation of himself to them, his chosen people, his intervention in their lives, above all in their liberation from slavery and in the covenant he made with them at Sinai. The psalms became hymns of praise and thanksgiving, and later developed into supplication and were used at their religious services. Their meal-prayers also expressed this note of praise and gratitude. Those prayers took on a special significance on the occasion of family gatherings, especially at the paschal festival. They became more or less a liturgy in themselves and had the atmosphere of a sacrifice.

We can outline the phases of the Paschal Supper. It opened with a ritual hand-washing. Then each one drank a first cup of wine, pronouncing this blessing: "Blessed be thou, our God, King of the universe, who givest us the fruit of the vine." This is the first cup mentioned by Saint Luke:

"Having taken the chalice he gave thanks and said: "Divide it among you, I will not drink of the fruit of the vine until the Kingdom of God comes" (22:18). The meal then began with the presiding one taking some bread, breaking it, and passing it around while saying the blessing: "Blessed be thou, our God, King of the universe, who bringest forth bread from the earth." It is probable that it was at this point that Christ pronounced the words of consecration over the bread. The various courses were then served, each introduced with a blessing. The paschal supper was distinguished for its special foods: bitter herbs and the paschal lamb. The one presiding explained the meaning of the different foods served. The sacrificial significance of the words of consecration over the bread was high-lighted by the eating of the paschal lamb. At the end of the meal a special ceremonial took place, the bringing in of the lamps, accompanied by a special blessing. When the lamps were lighted, a second washing of hands took place and it was at this point Christ arose and washed the feet of the apostles. Then the one presiding took a cup of wine mixed with water and invited all to join him in a special prayer of thanksgiving. This cup was called "The cup of benediction" (cfr. 1 Cor. 10:16). The presiding one then said: "Let us give thanks to the Lord our God," and all responded: "Blessed be he whose generosity has given us food and whose kindness has given us life." There then followed a series of thanksgiving prayers, three at least. These prayers are said to be of very ancient origin. The third prayer, the longest, refers to the redemptive action of God in earlier times (Exodus). It begs for renewal and that they might find fulfilment in the coming of the Messiah (petitions). In this prayer there is frequent use of the word; 'Memorial' (remembrance) and this implies a sense of continuity. This prayer was also used in the ritual of the temple sacrifices, showing that they regarded the paschal supper as having a sacrificial character. At this stage, as he passed around the 'chalice of benediction', Christ pronounced the words of consecration over the chalice adding the command: "Do this in memory of me." In passing it is interesting to note that the Jewish form of prayer (thanksgiving, praise) is visible in the writings of Saint Paul.

The subsequent development of the liturgy of the eucharist pertains to the history of the Mass; it would take us too far afield and be outside our general theme of the Paschal Mystery. We must be satisfied to take a brief look at our present day Eucharistic Prayers and see how the theme of praise, thanksgiving and supplication is included in them. Each of them is introduced by the Preface (part of the prayer). It opens with a dialogue between priest and people. The greeting: "The Lord be with you" is semitic in origin. The words: "Let us give thanks to the Lord our God" is taken from the Jewish Ritual. The theme of thanksgiving is then taken up. In the Eastern liturgies the themes are manifold and all expressed in one Preface. In the Roman Rite they are more condensed and divided out over the various seasons and feasts. In the new Roman Missal there are over eighty in all. If the specific themes were joined it would make a clear picture of salvation-history. The Preface concludes with the "Sanctus". As this was a later insertion it has tended to break the sequence of thought expressed in the Preface and to give the idea that the Preface is not part of the Eucharistic Prayer. But on a closer study the Prayer continues after the 'Sanctus' with the same thoughts as the Preface. The first Eucharistic Prayer (the Roman Canon) says: "We come to you, Father, with praise and thanksgiving;" the second one: "Lord, you are holy indeed;" the third one: "Father, you are holy indeed and all creation rightly gives you praise, all life, all holiness comes from you;" the fourth one: "Father, we acknowledge your greatness, all your actions show your wisdom.' In all four prayers we find not only praise and thanksgiving but also intercessions and petitions for the Church and its various

112

members, living and dead. In the Roman one these intercessions are divided, two before the consecration and two
after. In the other three all are placed at the very end of the
prayer, before the doxology. All four Eucharistic Prayers
contain the institution narrative, and the liturgical
proclamation, having the words of consecration as its heart
and core. It proclaims in word and action what Christ did at
the Last Supper. That is the assurance of the reality of the
presence of Christ's Paschal Mystery in the Mass. There is a
slight variation in the introductory words: "The day before
he suffered," "Before he was given up to death," "On the
night he was betrayed," "While they were at Supper." The
form of the actual words of consecration are composite,
taken from the various gospel traditions. The words
"Mysterium fidei" (Mystery of faith) have been taken out of
the wording for the consecration of the chalice and added
afterwards with an acclamation by the people. It is an act of
faith in the real presence of Christ, the victim. He is present
as he is now in heaven, in a glorified state. The separate
consecration of the bread and wine show forth the death of
the Lord in an unbloody or sacramental manner. There
follows what is known in all liturgies as the "Anamnesis", the
prayer of offering of the victim to the Father. All four
prayers express the reality of Christ's Paschal Mystery.
"Father, we celebrate the memory of Christ, your Son. We
recall his passion, his resurrection from the dead and his
ascension into glory. . . We offer you this holy and perfect
sacrifice" (E.P. 1). "In memory of his death and resurrection
we offer you, Father, this life-giving bread, this saving
cup" (E.P. 2). "Father, calling to mind the death your Son
endured for our salvation, his glorious resurrection and
ascension into heaven and ready to greet him when he
comes again, we offer you in thanksgiving this holy and
living sacrifice. Look with favour on your Church's offering
and see the victim whose death has reconciled us to
yourself" (E.P. 3). "Father, we now celebrate this memorial

of our redemption, . . . we offer you his body and blood, the acceptable sacrifice which brings salvation to the whole world. Look upon this sacrifice which you have given to your Church" (E.P. 4). Realising then that the reality of Christ's redemptive sacrifice is renewed in the Mass, is it any wonder the *Constitution* "Earnestly desires that all the faithful should be led to that full, conscious and active participation. . . Such participation by the Christian people, 'a chosen race, a royal priesthood, a holy nation, a redeemed people', is their right and duty by reason of their baptism." It also states: "From that time onwards (the first Pentecost) the Church has never failed to come together to celebrate the Paschal Mystery;. . . celebrating the eucharist in which "the victory and triumph of his death are again made present." Saint Athanasius expresses it in these words: "Whenever together we eat the Lord's flesh and drink his blood, we celebrate the Pasch." All four eucharistic prayers conclude with the same doxology, based on words from Saint Paul, Rm. 11:36 & Eph. 3:21. "Through him, with him, in him, in the unity of the Holy Spirit, all glory and honour is yours, almighty Father, for ever and ever." Through him, who is our Mediator (for we have an advocate with the Father, says Saint John), with him, who is our brother, for we are and are called sons of God, says the same Saint John, in him who is our Head, for we are members of his Mystical Body. Just as the people of old, as they celebrated the Paschal Feast, felt they were in some way united with its historical reality, so we, the new people of God, must not only realize with faith the reality of Calvary in the living present in the Mass but must also endeavour to unite ourselves with that sublime offering. That is the force of our response to the doxology. Our "Amen" is our ratification of all that has been done at the altar of sacrifice. It is not only our approval but our commitment to live in the spirit of that sacrifice.

It is of interest to realise that the eucharistic prayers,

particularly the three new ones, are ancient yet modern. They are ancient in so far as they have drawn on the tradition of ancient eucharistic prayers and adapted to modern needs. They link us with the past; we feel we are praying with the same words of past generations, even as far back as the third century and with phrases adopted from the ancient Jewish Ritual.

In conclusion a word about the Communion Rite for it is also a sharing in the Paschal Mystery. The *Constitution* says: "That more perfect form of participation in the Mass whereby the faithful, after the priest's communion, receive the Lord's body from the same sacrifice, is strongly recommended." [5] It also says: "In like manner as often as they eat the Supper of the Lord they proclaim the death of the Lord until he comes." [6] The Communion Rite has always been regarded as the completion of our participation in the renewal of the Paschal Mystery. The Postcommunion prayers outline for us the fruits of this eucharistic banquet, e.g., "Grant us, almighty God, that our souls may always retain the grace of the sacrament of your Son's death and resurrection."

The eucharist contains the whole mystery of Christ, his Paschal Mystery in its sacramental form. If we could only grasp the depth of this mystery of love in its threefold dimension, sacrifice, sacrament and abiding presence, if we could but "know this gift of God", as Christ said to the woman at the Well of Jacob. What we need is expressed in a phrase of the first eucharistic prayer, 'fides et devotio', faith and devotion.

1. C.L. 47.
2. idem. 51.
3. idem. 33.
4. idem. 48.
5. idem. 55.
6. idem. 6.

5. THE PASCHAL MYSTERY
AND THE OTHER SACRAMENTS

All the sacraments have their origin in the priestly sacrifice of Christ, his Paschal Mystery. Each sacrament pours out from the priestly hands of Christ its glorious fruits. In the sacraments then Christ takes our fundamental situations and desires, to raise them to a Christian level. It is Christ entering into our lives to enable us to share in his Paschal Mystery. The sacraments then aim at transforming us into the image of Christ and sanctify almost every stage and event in our lives. The *Constitution* points this out in the opening section of chapter three: "The purpose of the sacraments is to sanctify men, to build up the body of Christ and finally to give worship to God; because they are signs they also instruct. They not only presuppose faith, but by words and objects they also nourish, strengthen and express it; that is why they are called "sacraments of faith". They have indeed the power to impart grace [1]. . . The faithful have access to the stream of divine grace which flows from the Paschal Mystery of the passion, death and resurrection of Christ, the font from which the sacraments draw their power." [2] The first thing the *Constitution* draws our attention to, is not their administration or reception but their celebration: "The very act of celebrating them effectively disposes the faithful to receive this grace fruitfully." [3] In other words they are liturgical celebrations and as such are professions of faith. They are acts of worship and efficacious signs of sanctification. They draw their power from the Paschal Mystery. Since the eucharist is the memorial and renewal of this mystery there is a close link between the eucharist and the other sacraments. This is now more clear from the regulation that the sacraments (except penance) be celebrated within the framework of the Mass. This however is not essential. The link is also indicated from the fact that the oils used in some of the sacraments are blessed at the Mass of the Chrism on Holy Thursday. Penance however has its link, which was more evident in the ancient Mass for the Reconciliation of penitents, also on Holy Thursday. It is evident too from the fact that one in serious sin is excluded from participation in the eucharistic banquet until reconciled in the sacrament of penance. Baptism is linked with the Paschal Mystery, for "We are buried with him in order to rise with him and walk in newness of life" (Rm. 6:4). In the water which came forth from the side of Christ on the Cross, the Fathers of the Church see the symbol of the waters of baptism. Baptism incorporates us into the Body of Christ and makes us participate in his priesthood in different degrees, including sacred orders and what is referred to as the priesthood of the laity. Thereby it gives us the right to participate in the eucharist. The baptismal water is blessed during the Paschal Vigil. "By baptism men are plunged into the Paschal Mystery of Christ; they die with him, are buried with him and rise with him; they receive the spirit of adoption as sons "in which we cry: 'Abba, Father!' " (*Constitution*).

Confirmation imprints a new character on the soul, and more abundant graces to complete the grace of baptism. Confirmation is linked with the Eucharist in that the eucharist is the *food of the strong*, the nourishment of those whom confirmation has made virile Christians.

The sacrament of penance washes the soul in the blood of the lamb, shed on Calvary. It too points to the Eucharist, because it prepares the penitent to receive the blessed sacrament. The sacrament of the sick (no longer "Extreme Unction") unites the sick persons with the suffering Christ, whose merits strengthen the soul.

Holy Orders is most closely bound up with Calvary and the Eucharist. It was at the Last Supper that Christ instituted this sacrament when he conferred the priesthood of the New Law on his apostles, and enabled them to transmit this power to others.

Matrimony draws its inspiration from the sacrifice of Christ who espoused his Bride, the Church, on the Cross. The sacraments also have a community aspect in the active participation of the faithful in their celebration. This is very evident in the new rites. They envisage a full participation of the community. This had been the directive of the Council: In this restoration, both texts and rites should be drawn up so that they express more clearly the holy things which they signify; the Christian people, as far as possible, should be enabled to understand them with ease and take part in them fully and actively. The sacraments, because they are signs also instruct. To help the faithful to appreciate the meaning and value of the sacraments, passages from Sacred Scriptures are introduced into the sacramental rites, but these should be explained, because "It is from the scriptures that actions and signs derive their meaning" (art. 24). Baptism has the clearest link with the Paschal Mystery as can be seen from the sixth chapter of Saint Paul's letter to the Romans, from the liturgy of the Paschal Vigil and from patristic tradition. Baptism introduces new members into the Christian community, new people of God, born again of water and the Holy Spirit as Saint John says. Saint Paul sees it as "a new creation".

That Confirmation is closely linked is not as clear. However, it is clear enough from the fact that, in the early centuries, Confirmation was closely linked with Baptism and the Eucharist, and they were known as the *sacraments of*

Christian initiation. Confirmation is the perfecting of what baptism began, and in the new rite those about to be confirmed renew their baptismal promises. The Fathers also saw in Confirmation the fulfilment of some of the figures of the old covenant. Saint Cyril of Jerusalem sees the association with the Paschal Mystery, in that through Baptism the candidate is conformed to Christ in his death and resurrection, and in the fact that Confirmation, by the anointing of the Holy Spirit, enables one to bear witness to Christ. As in the natural order an adult differs from a child above all in his sense of responsibility, so also in the spiritual order, spiritual manhood calls for responsibility, for action, for cooperation. It calls upon the individual to be ready to defend the interests of Christ in his own soul and in the Church of which he is a member. At the same time Confirmation gives us the special grace of the Holy Spirit to carry out the duties that such responsibility entails. It gives us fortitude to fight as good soldiers of Christ, and to defend the rights and teaching of Christ, our King. This sacrament is preeminently the sacrament of the Holy Spirit.

The ancient liturgy of Lent, providing for the public penitents, was intimately associated with the celebration of the Paschal Mystery. The penitents were expelled from the Church on Ash Wednesday and reconciled with God and the Church on Holy Thursday in the special Mass of Reconciliation. The Liturgy of the word during Lent had as one of its themes that of repentance and mercy, and was directed to the penitents, who could be present just for that portion of the Mass. The Sacrament of Penance or "Reconciliation" (as the new rite calls it) can be regarded as a new paschal liberation for the penitent; for he is once more made clean in the blood of the lamb. The new form of this sacrament is very paschal in its wording. Worth noting is the fact that the sacrament was instituted by Christ on the day of his resurrection, when he completed his Paschal Mystery. The new rite stresses the note of reconciliation both with

God and with the Church. It envisages a threefold form: the reconciliation of individual penitents, the reconciliation of many penitents but with individual confession, and the reconciliation of many penitents with a general absolution. This last is only for exceptional cases and the obligation of individual confession of grave sin still holds and must be fulfilled later. In the second and third forms the rite is introduced by a communal penitential rite. The sacrament of the Anointing of the Sick is closely linked with the Paschal Mystery. Its purpose is to bring to perfection the initial paschal victory over Satan in baptism. It brings health to soul and body. It remits sin, and this is itself a paschal work. While essentially a sacrament of the sick, it has close associations with one's final illness, which is for each of us a "passover" from this world to the Father. As such it disposes the sick person to become like Christ in his acceptance of his passover to the Father. This fact should give us a fresh and truly faith-filled Christian outlook on the problem of sickness and human suffering. *The solution is to be found in Christ.* By our baptism we are committed to become like him, conformed to the image of the Suffering Saviour. We are one in suffering with him, and from that unity we draw strength, courage and grace to accept and bear our illnesses and sufferings. Saint Paul has this in mind when he speaks of filling up what is wanting in the sufferings of Christ. Not that there is anything wanting in Christ's sufferings, but he, as our Head, has left to us, his members, a sharing in his sufferings by our carrying our cross with love and patience as he did. Life here below is not everything; we are only pilgrims and indeed our sufferings are light and passing in comparison with the glory to come. A prayerful study of the new rite of this sacrament in all its details will help everyone to view it in a Christ-like manner and will be a source of encouragement to receive it in our hour of sickness. If people were so anxious to receive bodily health from Christ when he lived on earth why should we not be anxious to receive that same help from the special sacrament that he has left to us for this purpose? The sacrament of Holy Orders is very much linked with the Paschal Mystery, its institution at the Last Supper, by the power to forgive sin involved and by the command to go forth and preach. The ministers of this sacrament are dispensers of the Mystery of Christ. They share in the priesthood of Christ in a more intimate way than the ordinary faithful and they exercise that priesthood most of all in the celebration of the holy Eucharist. Matrimony also shares in the Paschal Mystery. Its link derives from the union between Christ and his Spouse (the Church) effected on the Cross. This image is the perfect model of the union between husband and wife. Saint Paul refers to the fact in his letter to the Ephesians. Marriage is a union of love but there is no true love without sacrifice. "Husbands love your wives just as Christ loved the Church and delivered himself up for it; that he might sanctify it. . . This is a great sacrament" (Eph. 5:25-26,33). The family, the fruit of the marriage union, is, as the *Constitution on the Church* says: "a miniature church".

Thus the whole sacramental system is closely bound up with Christ's redemptive work, achieved by his Paschal Mystery and now applied to the souls of men in and through the liturgy of the sacraments, thereby helping to build up his Body, the Church. Through the liturgy of the sacraments the realities of the supernatural order become clear. Recalling such facts in the natural order as birth, growth, renewal, fruitfulness, a returning to the source, one becomes aware that these things are made spiritually real in the sacraments. We can look at the sacraments from a triple point of view; the past, Christ's Paschal Mystery, the source and cause of his merits and grace; the present, the infusion or increase of that divine life into souls; and the future, the glory of heaven. So through the sacraments Christ is continuing his divine mission of sanctifying souls, giving them the opportunity of keeping in contact with him and glorifying the Father. Each sacrament has its own particular grace conformable to the end for which it was instituted and so each one gives us the right to the appropriate graces as we need them throughout our lives. It is important to remember this especially in regard to the sacraments we receive only once. It is through the sacraments that we are grafted on to the Vine as living branches. We are strengthened, pruned and restored to health. From them we receive the continual sap of divine life to help us grow unto the fulness of Christ, who is the true Vine. Through the sacramental system Christ's Paschal Mystery is ever active and fruitful in the life of his Church and its members. We must see the sacraments in that light and not as just isolated helps at our disposal at various times in life. The sacraments are not solely a personal relationship between Christ and the individual. They are sacraments *of the Church* and sacraments *of faith.*

1. C.L. 59.
2. idem. 61.
3. idem. 59.

6. THE PASCHAL MYSTERY AND THE LITURGICAL YEAR

A. INTRODUCTION

In his Apostolic letter, introducing the New Calendar (1969), Pope Paul VI wrote: "The influence of the Paschal Mystery on each day, each week, and the whole course of the year shows us that the Paschal Mystery is at the heart of the whole Liturgical Year. This must be evident in the various seasons and in the feasts of the saints." The Letter also stated: "The celebration of the Liturgical Year exerts a special sacramental power and influence which strengthens the Christian Life."

In his Encyclical *Mediator Dei*, Pope Pius XII wrote: "All the year round the celebration of the eucharistic mystery and the recitation of the Divine Office revolve about the person of Christ [1]... The sacred liturgy seeks to make the faithful share in them in such a way that the divine Head of the Mystical Body lives by his perfect holiness in each of his members [2]. . . The Liturgical Year is no cold lifeless representation of past events, no mere historical record. It is Christ himself, living on in his Church and still pursuing the path of boundless mercy. These mysteries are still constantly present and active." (3) The *Constitution on the Sacred Liturgy* is no less clear: "Holy Mother Church considers it her duty to celebrate the saving work of her divine Spouse by devoutly recalling it to mind on certain days throughout the course of the year. . . As each year passes by, she unfolds the whole mystery of Christ, from the Incarnation and birth until the Ascension, the day of Pentecost and the expectation of blessed hope and of the coming of the Lord... Reflecting thus upon the mysteries of redemption, the Church opens to the faithful the riches of her Lord's powers and merits, so that these are in some way made present for all time and the faithful are enabled to lay hold upon them and become filled with saving grace." (4) The celebration of the Liturgical Year is the celebration of the history and economy of salvation which has its apex in the solemnity of the Pasch. It goes without saying that the liturgical cycle owes its formation to the Holy Spirit who directs the Church. Each feast commemorates and renews the unique mystery of salvation under a particular light. This it does, not in isolation, but in relation to the whole mystery of salvation. That explains the constant use of the word 'hodie' (today) in the various seasons and feasts. This also shows us that the Liturgical Year is paschal, as Louis Bouyer points out: (5) "Easter is the centre where all the liturgy converges, and the spring from whence it flows." He also says: "In the Liturgical Year the Mystery of Christ is proclaimed, communicated and participated in." Furthermore is not the Eucharistic Sacrifice the very centre of every feast, of every season, of every celebration? Every Mass contains the whole mystery of Christ and every Mass is the central point of every celebration during the year.

For Saint Paul the mystery of Christ is the revelation of God in Christ. The Fathers of the Church speak of the power of the mystery in liturgical celebrations. Saint Leo says: "What is visible in the Lord has passed over into the mysteries". "I find you in the mysteries," writes Saint

124

Ambrose. It is the Eucharist that makes actual the presence of the mystery. The fact that the whole mystery of Christ, past, present and future, is contained in each celebration gives meaning to the various seasons and feasts. Our capacity for grasping the whole mystery at once is limited; we cannot fathom all at once the riches of the graces in the mystery of Christ. We have, as it were, to take this mystery apart, analyse its various aspects, and so concentrate our attention on one aspect at a time so as to become more and more permeated with its full meaning. That is what each season and each feast does for us. The whole is built into the framework of the Paschal Mystery. The Liturgical Year more or less takes the events of the Mystery of Christ in chronological order and concentrates our attention on the doctrine, the beauty and example of that particular aspect. That is why the *Constitution* goes on to say: "The Liturgical Year is to be revised so that the traditional customs and training methods of the sacred seasons shall be preserved or else restored. . . their specific character is to be retained, so that they duly nourish the piety of the faithful who celebrate the mysteries of Christian redemption, especially the Paschal Mystery." (6) The Liturgical Year consecrates the ordinary solar year as 'The Year of the Lord' because the mystery of salvation embraces the whole of Christ's life; its preparation in the Old Testament, its reality in the New Testament, and its promulgation in the life of the Church.

Thus in the course of the year we have a new epiphany, a new manifestation, under the veil of signs, of the Incarnate Word of God, the Word made flesh, living like us, immolated for us, raised from the dead and glorified for us. That is why the *Constitution* could write: "To accomplish so great a work, Christ is always present in his Church, especially in her liturgical actions. . . Christ indeed always associates the Church with himself in this great work wherein God is perfectly glorified and men are sanctified. The liturgy is then rightly considered as an exercise of the priestly office of Jesus Christ." [7] So the seasons and feasts of the Liturgical Year are not just pious actions which represent historical events in some dramatic way. No, they have as their object to produce the effects in us of these mysteries. Hence Dom Gueranger in his introduction to *The Liturgical Year*, wrote: "It is Jesus himself who is the source as well as the object of his mysteries in the Church and in the faithful soul. . . Each year the Church sees him as an infant in the manger, fasting in the desert, offering himself on the cross, rising from the grave, founding his Church, instituting the sacraments, ascending to the right hand of the Father and sending the Holy Spirit upon men. The graces of all these divine mysteries are renewed in her. . . What the Liturgical Year does for the Church at large, it does also for the soul of each one of the faithful who is careful to receive the gift of God." In *Mediator Dei* Pius XII wrote: "The liturgy presents Christ to us not only as an example to imitate but as a teacher for us to believe, as a shepherd for us to follow, as an advocate who saves us, as the source of our holiness and as the mystical Head, whose members we are and whose life we live [8]. . . His mysteries live in us in their effects, since each of them is, according to its nature and in its own way, the cause of our salvation." [9] That is why he also wrote that "these mysteries are still now constantly present and active so that the souls of men might come in contact with them and so live by them." [10] The natural cycle of our lives is a symbol of what our supernatural lives ought to be through our participation in the mystery of Christ. In the natural order we are born, are given life and must nourish and take care of that life. The same is true of our supernatural lives. We were originally reborn through our contact with the mystery of Christ when we received Baptism. We must develop, care for and nourish that divine life, and this we do especially in our contact with Christ in the eucharist. Again, just as our natural life grows in time, year by year, so does our

Christian life, when the Church presents the chief phases of the mystery of Christ in the Liturgical Year. We must strive to relive those mysteries in our own life, day by day and year by year, until Christ be formed in us. We are aware that our natural life has a limit and will come to an end at death. Similarly with our Christian life: our daily participation in the Mystery of Christ will not be an unending cycle. It too will come to an end at the time of our natural death, but it will not cease to exist, it will give birth to the new life of glory. The more we endeavour to live our Christian lives with the Church as she lives her Liturgical Year, the greater will be the glory we render to God the Father and the greater our union with Christ, our Head, His Son. To draw fruit from the 'Year of Grace' it may help to dwell at somewhat greater length on the various seasons and feasts of the year. The order outlined in the fifth chapter of the *Constitution on the Sacred Liturgy* will be followed.

B. THE PASCHAL MYSTERY AND SUNDAY

The Lord's Day is the original feast day to be proposed to the piety of the faithful. In the fifth chapter of the *Constitution on the Sacred Liturgy* we read: "Every week, on the day which she has called The Lord's Day, she keeps the memory of her Lord's resurrection. (11) By a tradition handed down from the apostles and going back to the very day of Christ's resurrection, the Church celebrates the Paschal Mystery every eighth day; with good reason this then bears the name of the Lord's Day or Sunday". On this day Christ's faithful should come together into one place so that, by hearing the word of God and taking part in the Eucharist, they may call to mind the passion, resurrection and glorification of the Lord Jesus and thank God who 'has begotten them again, through the resurrection of Jesus Christ from the dead, unto a living hope' (1 Pt. 1:3). The phrase, "The Lord's Day" is found both in the Old and the New Testaments, and usually refers to the intervention of God in history. When applied to Sunday it not only recalls the triumph of Christ over Satan, the day also which crowned the work of Christ by the sending of the Holy Spirit, but it is the day consecrated by Christians to divine worship. There is a link between the Lord's Day and the Mass, which is the heart and centre of Catholic worship, bringing us into direct and life-giving contact with the Paschal Mystery of Christ. The Sunday has always been regarded as the weekly celebration of the Paschal Mystery. Strange as it may seem, this weekly celebration is more ancient than the annual celebration at Easter. We read in the Acts of the Apostles (20:7) Saint Paul's reference to this weekly celebration; "On the first day of the week when we had met for the breaking of bread." The saints and writers of the first centuries all refer to the sacredness of the Sunday. Saint Ignatius of Antioch writes: "They do not observe Saturday, the Sabbath, any more. Instead they observe Sunday, the day on which a new life was given us by Christ through his death and resurrection." He also designated the Christian as "the one who celebrated Sunday". Tertullian calls Sunday "the day of the resurrection". Again we read in the second century: "You shall assemble on the first day of the week, the Lord's Day, break bread and give thanks in order that your sacrifice may be pure." Saint Justin (also 2nd century) opens his detailed account of the Sunday celebration with the words: "On the day which is called the Day of the Sun, an assembly takes place. We assemble on the Day of the Sun because it is the first day of the week, because on this day Jesus Christ rose from the dead." Again from that period we read: "In happiness we spend this eighth day on which Christ arose, and, having manifested himself, ascended to heaven." The Sunday is here called the eighth day. It is not only the first day of the week, the dawn of a new world initiated by the risen Christ but it is also the eighth day, a day that goes beyond the seven days of the week and in so doing becomes a symbol of the day beyond the days, the day without decline in eternity, the day of the repose of God. Sunday reminds us of our true destiny and, because it is an anticipated joy, it should be celebrated in a festive and joyful manner. It highlights our liberation, the fact that we are no longer slaves, but free and children of God our Father, with whom we hope to live for all eternity. So Sunday is truly "The Lord's Day", the day we devote to him in prayer and worship. In the fourth century Eusebius wrote: "We the children of the New Covenant celebrate our Pasch every Sunday, being always nourished by the Body of the Saviour and always partaking of the Blood of the Lamb. Every week on the Lord's Day we observe the feast of the Pasch, celebrating the mysteries of the true Lamb by whom we were redeemed." The early monks and hermits always left their solitude to celebrate in common the Sunday. Saint Basil says: "On Sunday we pray standing, in order to remind ourselves that we shall rise with Christ." In the fifth century this bond of unity on the Sunday and its celebration was expressed in what was called "the fermentum". This was a portion of the Host consecrated by the Pope at Mass and sent by him to priests who could not come to his celebration, because of their own celebration. It was also sent from the Stational Mass on the weekdays of Lent. This sending of a particle of the sacred Host was a symbol of the unity of people in the same divine worship, and among themselves. Pope Innocent I said it was the day when unity was strengthened all the more. He also added that he was expressing an ancient tradition in the words "Easter happiness illumines every Sunday". After the era of persecution the Sunday, under Constantine, became a day of rest, a day free from work in memory of all our Saviour had done. "It should be observed after the manner in which the Sabbath had previously been observed." According to Eusebius, the Emperor prescribed this so that the Christians would have the opportunity they need to engage in religious worship on the day which is called "The Day of Light or the Day of the Sun, and so be able to devote themselves to prayer." It is only in the sixth century however, that we find the precept of abstaining from servile work on Sunday. The reason then given is the same: "In order that the Christians may more easily attend Mass and devote themselves to prayer."

Now what message has this short review of the place Sunday has always held in the Church and in the lives of Christians?

First of all it reminds us of our duty to sanctify the Lord's Day and express our gratitude to Christ for his Paschal Mystery, whereby we were redeemed. Secondly we should strengthen our faith in its renewal in our Sunday Mass our "little Easter Day". Thirdly we should recall to mind the sentiments which ought to be ours at Sunday Mass.

The *Constitution* expresses it thus: "Mother Church desires that all the faithful should be led to that full, conscious and active participation. . . such participation by the Christian people, as a chosen race, a royal priesthood, a holy nation, a redeemed people, is their right and their duty by reason of their baptism. . . It is the primary and indispensable source from which the faithful are to derive the true Christian spirit [13]. . . Therefore when present at this mystery of faith, Christ's followers should not be there as strangers or silent spectators; on the contrary they should take part in the sacred action, conscious of what they are doing, with devotion. . . They should learn to offer themselves through Christ their Mediator." [14] Later on it also says in speaking of the revision of the Rite of the Mass that "it should be done in such a way that the intrinsic nature and purpose of its several parts may be more clearly manifested and that devout and active participation by the people may be achieved." (15) Now with the New Rite of the Mass, including the vernacular, such participation should be more than a possibility, it should be a reality. This reality does not seem to be achieved. The sad fact is, that many neglect their Sunday Mass, and complain of boredom or lack of interest. Is it a lack of faith in what the Mass really is that is the cause? It is hard to imagine lack of interest or boredom if one believes the Mass is the renewal of our redemption. Such an attitude was not the spirit of the early Christians, nor the spirit which animated our forefathers. Are not our historic Mass Rocks a testimony of their appreciation and loyalty to the Mass? It is the heritage we have received and at what a cost! Will we fail to pass on that heritage? Only faith, love and appreciation of what the Mass is, will assure our passing it on.

C. THE PASCHAL MYSTERY AND THE FESTIVAL OF THE PASCH

"Once a year, by the most solemn festival of the Pasch, she celebrates his resurrection together with his blessed passion." (16) So the *Constitution* speaks of the annual feast of the Pasch. The very first feast (after that of Sunday) was Easter, the Sacred Triduum of the Pasch. It is the most ancient season or period of the Liturgical Year, dating from apostolic times. For the first four centuries it was celebrated as a unit, passion, death and resurrection. This unity began to disappear with the celebration of a double Triduum, Holy

Thursday to Holy Saturday and Easter Sunday to Easter Tuesday. Later the paschal festival was extended to the whole of Holy Week and all of Easter Week. During this period there was no work. Later on in the late Middle Ages a further change was brought about, primarily on the question of work. North of the Alps this was the period of sowing, and so it was difficult to stop work for so long. Another change was also introduced, the anticipating of the morning ceremonies rather than their celebration at the times at which the actual events took place. This helped to make the double Triduum clear-cut, the first (Holy Thursday to Holy Saturday) recalled Christ's passion and death and the second (Sunday to Tuesday) his resurrection. This more or less led to a disunity in the manner of the celebration. The reform of Holy Week (1955) aimed at restoring the original Triduum, the Sacred Triduum from Holy Thursday evening to Easter Sunday morning (at least after midnight). The entire liturgy of Holy Week or 'the Great Week' as Saint John Chrysostom calls it, places before us not only in words, but with all the expressiveness of sublime and dramatic ceremonial, the events of Christ's Paschal Mystery from his entry into Jerusalem on the Sunday to his resurrection on the following Sunday morning. In that time during the first Holy Week, Christ accomplished his Paschal Mystery: "For us and for our salvation. . . He suffered under Pontius Pilate, was crucified, died and was buried. The third day he rose from the dead." Such is our profession of faith in that mystery as we express it in the Creed at Mass. During Holy Week we relive in every detail his Paschal Mystery. The whole of Holy Week forms a unity, all leading up to the great Paschal Vigil on Holy Saturday night. Holy Week opens on the Sunday we now call the *Sunday of the Passion* or *Palm Sunday*. On that day we re-enact the triumphal entry of Christ into Jerusalem. The procession on that first Palm Sunday was the solemn entry of the great high Priest into the Holy of holies to offer his sacrifice. It was the march of the King of kings into the field of battle. Red is the colour used on this day, because it is the symbol of the bloody conflict he is about to engage in against the prince of darkness. On this day we take part in the blessing of the palms and in the solemn procession of the palms to the church, the new Jerusalem. We thereby pledge and renew our loyalty to Christ, our King. In the Mass which follows we listen to the history of the passion from one of the synoptic gospels. The liturgy of the next three days centres on the theme of the Passion. Saint Matthew has left us much of the teaching given by Christ during those, his last days. Thursday of this week is called Holy Thursday because of the sacred events which took place on that day. For many centuries there were three masses on this day; one in the early morning for the reconciliation of the penitents who were doing public penance during Lent. Later on there was a mass for the blessing of the oils to be used in the administration of the sacraments, especially at the Paschal Vigil. The third mass in the late evening, was the beginning of the Sacred Triduum... It was the Mass of the Last Supper. The first mass fell into disuse when the practice of public penance ceased, the other two were joined and celebrated in the morning. This was one of the reasons for thinking Holy Thursday was part of the Triduum. Now, in the restored Rite, the Mass of the blessing of the Oils, the Mass of the Chrism, is celebrated in the morning and the Mass of the Lord's Supper in the evening and that is the opening of the Sacred Triduum, the Paschal Festival. In imitation of Christ's washing the feet of his disciples, provision is now made for this ablution at the evening Mass, after the homily. After the Mass the blessed sacrament is taken in solemn procession to the altar of repose to receive the homage and gratitude of the faithful for the triple gift Christ gave us on that first Holy Thursday night, the eucharistic sacrifice, and sacrament, and the priesthood of the New Law, all of which issued from the

Heart of our Priest and Saviour. The adoration at the altar of Repose ends at midnight.

On Good Friday the Church in her liturgy of the Passion and Death of Christ recalls the tragedy of Calvary. The altar, the symbol of Christ, is absolutely bare, as he was on the Cross. There is a deep sense of mourning but with a sorrow that has its note of joy. The liturgy is celebrated in the early afternoon to harmonise with the time of his death. It is the one day in the year when mass is not celebrated. The first part of the function is the liturgy of the word in its earliest form. The story of the Passion is taken from Saint John. This is followed by the unveiling and the "adoration" of the Cross. It is here that the note of joy and victory are echoed. The function concludes with the Communion Rite. This Rite was introduced only in the seventh century and from the late Middle Ages on was confined to the celebrant. In the New Order of Holy Week it is once more restored to all.

Holy Saturday is a day of mourning at the tomb while we await the Paschal Vigil that night. The Paschal Vigil is not only the climax of the Sacred Triduum but of the whole season of Lent and of the whole year. Saint Augustine has called it the mother of all vigils. There is a danger that we may miss the full significance of the Paschal Vigil (and the Paschal Season also) if we call them the Easter Vigil and Eastertide. The word Easter comes from an old English word 'eastre', meaning the goddess of spring. The English language is the only one that has not some form of the word Pasch. As a result, our word Easter does not capture the historical background of the festival. That may account for the fact that the faithful have not grasped or entered into it with enthusiasm.

It may be useful to recall the essential triple theme of the Paschal Vigil:

(1) the passage of the Hebrew people from captivity to freedom,

(2) the passage of Christ from death to life in his resurrection,

(3) the passage of the Christian from sin to grace through baptism.

The eastern liturgy expresses it thus: "People rejoice, it is the Pasch, the Pasch of the Lord, from death to life, Christ-God has led us from earth to heaven, Christ is risen." Christ's Paschal Mystery is the epitome of the Christian life; it contains all Christianity within itself.

The Paschal Vigil opens with the blessing of the fire and the Paschal Candle. This large candle, a symbol of the risen Christ, is also a symbol of the pillar of fire which went before the chosen people on their journey from Egypt. As the procession, headed by the lighted Candle, proceeds into the darkened church we hear the triple chant, "Christ our Light." There then follows the canticle of praise in honour of the risen Christ and his victory (the Exsultet). In this canticle we have many references to the original Pasch and the exodus of the chosen people. The hymn has been described as the most beautiful piece of theology ever written on the Paschal Mystery. It contains the whole message of Easter. The next section of the Vigil, a remnant of the ancient Vigil, consists of a series of readings from the Old Testament, recalling such events as creation, the sacrifice of Abraham, the safe passage through the Red Sea, and some passages from the prophets, foreshadowing baptism. The prayer which follows each reading points out how those symbols in the Old Testament are now fulfilled in the Christian Pasch. Between those readings and the readings from the New Testament the "Gloria" is intoned and the bells are once more rung. The first reading from the New Testament is from Saint Paul, showing that baptism is the Christian Pasch, our Passover from death to life, a new creation. The gospel is that of the resurrection of Christ from the tomb, reminding us again of our resurrection to the new life of grace through baptism. The Mass is interrupted at this stage for the liturgy of baptism, with the blessing of the water followed by the administration of the sacrament. If there is no baptismal font this ceremony is omitted. However Holy Water is blessed and the congregation, holding lighted candles, renew their baptismal promises. The Mass of the resurrection then continues in the usual way. If adults have been baptised, they may also be confirmed and make their first communion at this Mass, thereby receiving at the Paschal Vigil the three sacraments of initiation into the Christian way of life. In the Paschal Vigil we have the achievement of the ancient Pasch in the risen Christ, in the newly baptised, and in the rest of the faithful who renew their own baptism. Each Paschal Vigil should thus be a new beginning.

D. PREPARATION FOR THE PASCH. . . LENT

So important is the annual Festival of the Pasch that the Church has always found it necessary to set aside a period of preparation. This period we call Lent. The *Constitution* says: "The season of Lent has a twofold character: primarily by recalling or preparing for baptism and penance; it disposes the faithful who persevere in hearing the word of God and in prayer, to celebrate the Paschal Mystery. Hence: more use is to be made of the baptismal features proper to the lenten liturgy. . . the same applies to the penitential elements. . . It is important to impress on the minds of the faithful not only the social consequences of sin but also the essence of the virtue of penance. . . During Lent penance should not only be internal and individual but also external and social." (17) The word 'Lent' comes from an old English word 'lenten', meaning spring. The Lenten season more or less coincides with the season of Spring. The Latin term for Lent is 'Quadragesima', meaning forty, and recalling the forty days' fast of Christ in the desert, also the forty days' fast of Moses and Elias and the forty days' preaching of Jonas in the city of Nineveh. It signifies a long time. The length of the period has varied. In the third century the Lenten season was three weeks. Later it was extended to forty days. Fasting was a later addition. Since there was no fast on Sundays, Lent began four days earlier and the two days of the Triduum, Friday and Saturday, were included to make forty fasting days. As there are only two obligatory fast days now, the number forty is counted from Ash Wednesday to Holy Thursday before the Evening Mass. The Sundays are still not counted among the forty days. When we approach the study of the liturgy of Lent, it is essential to remember that in the earlier centuries the liturgy (as the *Constitution* points out) catered for two classes of souls. The first were those preparing for baptism at the Paschal Vigil. Much of the Lenten instruction in the Masses was directed to them. We, who have already been regenerated in the waters of baptism, can still find these instructions most useful to remind us of the duties and of the obligations that baptism places on us. The second class of souls specially catered for in the Lenten liturgy were the penitents, i.e., those who were doing public penance and preparing to be reconciled on Holy Thursday. This gives the key to many of the Readings in the Lenten Masses. We are not public penitents, neither is there public penance in the Church today, but we are sinners and must atone for our sins, and so we are required to do penance. From the eleventh century, public penance fell into disuse but the custom was retained of placing ashes on the heads of all the faithful on Ash Wednesday to remind them of their sins and of the punishment for sin. With this background, it is not surprising to find emphasized in the lenten liturgy those truths which we call the eternal truths; a frequent theme is the call to penance and self-denial. If one were asked what is the most characteristic note of Lent from the point of view of the Church, one word gives the answer: mercy. How often during the season we beg God for pardon and mercy. If some of the readings speak to us of bodily death, they also symbolise the death of the soul through sin. As instruction for those preparing for baptism such themes as faith, unbelief, grace are found throughout the lenten masses. We see then that the Church takes great care to prepare us to celebrate the great feast of the Pasch. The climax each day of that preparation is the daily celebration of the special mass prescribed for that individual day of Lent.

E. THE PROLONGATION OF THE PASCH. . . PASCHAL TIME

Just as there are nearly seven weeks of preparation for the Paschal Feast, so there are seven weeks spent in its celebration. Paschal Time extends· from Easter Sunday to Pentecost Sunday. It is the season of joy, joy at the triumph and victory of Christ, joy in the contemplation of the new life of grace acquired in baptism. To intensify this joy, the Church multiplies the recitation and chant of the shout of joy 'Alleluia'. Christ has risen, nature is reborn and man comes spiritually to life. It all speaks to us of the triple resurrection; the symbolic one in nature around us, the historical one which took place in Jerusalem, and the spiritual one in our souls. Easter is our spiritual birthday, because it recalls the day of our baptism, when we were reborn as children of God, our Father. We were nearly all baptised as infants and so, unlike the Christians of earlier centuries, we do not realise the wonders of our spiritual birth. They were adults when they received baptism at the Paschal Vigil, and for them each Paschal Vigil was a reminder and a renewal. A fresh commitment to our baptismal promises at the Vigil should be the high point of the celebration for us.

The special masses for the Octave of Easter and the Sunday masses of Paschal Time are a continuation of instruction for the newly baptised. The beauty of the new life they have received is stressed. The sense of charity, and the bond of union with one another as members of Christ, placed before them, are read in these masses today. The Acts of the Apostles tell us of the life of the infant Church. From the fourth century a feast in honour of the Ascension has been celebrated. If the Paschal Feast is a feast of faith, the Ascension is one of hope: Christ has promised that where he is now, in glory, we too will be one day.

The season closes with the solemnity of Pentecost, the feast of the Holy Spirit. This feast had its symbolic forerunner also in the Old Law. Fifty days after the feast of the Pasch, the Jews had their Pentecost, the feast of weeks. Originally it was a harvest festival when the first fruits were offered to God, but later a commemoration of the giving of the Law on Sinai became the object of the celebration. The word 'Pentecost' means in Greek, the fiftieth day. The Church has kept this feast as the close of the Paschal Season certainly since the second century and perhaps even earlier. For us it is the feast of the Coming of the Holy Spirit on the Apostles and the giving of the New Law, not on tablets of stone but in the hearts of men, the Law of love. It is the feast of love. "The love of God has been poured into our hearts by the Holy Spirit who has been given us" (Rm. 5:5). It is the day on which we recall our reception of the Holy Spirit at Confirmation, and we should renew the grace of that sacrament by begging for a fresh outpouring of the Holy Spirit into our souls. The Paschal season thus stresses the theological virtues: faith, hope and love.

F. THE PASCHAL MYSTERY AND THE CHRISTMAS SEASON

There is one other important season celebrated in the Liturgical Year, the Christmas season with its preparatory period of Advent. It is the season of preparation for and the celebration of the coming of Him who is to be the true Paschal Lamb, who shall take away the sins of the world.

Can we enter into the Advent-Christmas Cycle and participate in the birth of Christ as we do in his death and resurrection? No, except in so far as it leads us to the Paschal Mystery. The *Constitution* gives us the meaning òf this season when it says: "Within the cycle of the year, she (the Church) unfolds the whole mystery of Christ, not only from his incarnation and birth but also. . . the expectation of blessed hope and of the coming of the Lord." [18] This season then looks at the wonderful manifestation of the Lord's coming among us. The very word 'Epiphany' means manifestation. The Church does not of course confine her attention to that first coming, she looks forward in hope to the final coming of the Lord in glory at the end of time. The two comings of Christ are interwoven in the liturgy of the whole season. But another coming still, another Advent, is also envisaged—this time a spiritual one to the soul of each person. The historical coming is long past and cannot be renewed, but the Church draws our attention to the other two. The first advent was one in the weakness of human flesh, the final coming will be in power and glory. In between is that spiritual, hidden coming, our sharing in his life.

This spiritual coming is not confined to Christmas. His first coming to the soul is at baptism. He renews the grace of that visitation each time we receive a sacrament. In the Mass his coming has a double aspect; his coming in the liturgy of the word and his coming in the eucharistic mystery. We often speak of sickness and suffering as a visitation from God, and it is one, because he then comes to invite us to share in his suffering. He comes to us too in the person of our neighbour. He comes to us in the time of prayer. All these comings are spiritual visitations to renew or increase our sharing in his life so that we may be ready to greet him "when he comes in glory" at the end.

When the liturgy of Christmas speaks to us of a new birth, it means, therefore, a new outpouring of grace, of divine life to our souls. The incarnation and birth of Christ were all part of the single mission given to him by his Father. So we must view his life as a whole. His incarnation and birth rendered God visible in the person of His divine Son. Not only visible but passable, that is, a subject for suffering and death. It was also at the moment of his incarnation that he was anointed priest and that he himself accepted the role of being the victim that as a priest he would himself offer in sacrifice. This theme of the redemption is mentioned over and over again in the Christmas Liturgy, e.g., in the readings from St. Paul to Titus in the midnight Mass and Mass of the Dawn and in the gospel of the midnight Mass, where we read: "This day is born to you a Saviour."

The Son of man sanctified every stage of human life and merited grace at each stage as he lived that life for us and for our salvation. The value of each stage, each aspect, came from the fact that he who lived this life was a divine person. Every step was a step on the road to Calvary, to his death and resurrection. In that way Christmas and the Incarnation are linked with the Paschal Mystery from the fact that the Mass is the centre of each day's celebration throughout the whole season. Christ's birth is the beginning of that life-work which was to bring us back to the Father. While the liturgy of this season celebrates the first coming of Christ, she also lays stress on his final coming. While the Church seems to live again in spirit those long centuries of expectation and longing when she places on our lips those prayers of longing for the coming of the Messiah, she is doing so to remind us of the need we all have of the Christ. We should not forget that the chosen people had in mind the coming of the Kingdom of God, the destruction of the powers of evil, all the symbols of the messianic age. This will occur only when he comes again in glory and all things will be subject to him. The idea of this final Advent runs through the liturgy of the Christmas season, e.g., the two passages from Saint Paul's letters to Titus: "Looking forward for the blessed hope and coming in glory of the great God and our Saviour, Jesus Christ, who gave himself for us that he might redeem us from all iniquity" (Tit. 2:13-14); "He saved us by the laver of regeneration (baptism)... that being justified by his grace we may be heirs according to hope in life everlasting" (Tit. 3:5-7). The prayers also speak of his being "the author of our new life, and the giver of immortality". In reminding us of the final advent of Christ the Church is telling us that "we have not here a lasting city"; we are seeking one that is to come. She is stirring up our hope in the life to come and making us realise the true meaning of our Christian life. Each spiritual advent of Christ to the soul is a new out-pouring of grace to help us on our pilgrim's way, back to our Father's home, in heaven.

Advent has been influenced by Lent, it is of later origin. We find this influence in the East, for example, as a special time of baptism at the Epiphany. The length of the period, like Lent, varied. In the early Middle Ages it was forty days, starting on November 11th. Fasting was a notable factor at that period but later the total period was reduced to four Sundays, and the fast was confined to the Quarter Tense Days and the Eve of Christmas.

The Liturgy today celebrates the Christmas festival from December 25th to January 13th. The East celebrated it on January 6th. Later East and West exchanged their feasts and the West made January 6th the Feast of the Epiphany—the manifestation of the Saviour-King, to the whole world in the person of the Magi. In the liturgy of this feast we also find overtones of Christ's final coming. The whole of Advent-Christmas season is rich in content and provides ample food for thought and reflection and is our first step in following Christ towards his Paschal Mystery.

1. M.D. 162.
2. idem. 163.
3. idem. 176.
4. C.L. 102.
5. The Paschal Mystery. London 1951.
6. C.L. 107.
7. C.L. 7.
8. M.D. 174.
9. idem. 176.
10. idem. 176.
11. idem. 102.
12. idem. 106.
13. idem. 14.
14. idem. 48.
15. idem. 50.
16. idem. 102.
17. idem. 109, 110.
18. idem. 102.

7. THE PASCHAL MYSTERY AND
OUR LADY

The unique place occupied by Our Lady in the work of the redemption of the human race called for a corresponding place in the liturgical year. The honour and cult which the Church has paid to Mary is even more ancient than her place in the liturgy. Speaking of the liturgical year the *Constitution on the Sacred Liturgy* says: "In celebrating this annual cycle of Christ's mysteries, Holy Church honours with especial love the Blessed Mary, Mother of God, who is inseparably involved in the saving work of her Son. In her the Church admires and holds up the most perfect fruit of the redemption, and joyfully contemplates, as in a faultless image, that which she herself desires and hopes wholly to be." [1] This quotation makes it clear that none entered so fully into participation in the Paschal Mystery of Christ as did she, his Mother.

What we might call the first intimation of the Paschal Mystery was made by God himself in the Genesis story of Eden: the promise of the woman and her seed who would crush the serpent's head. That woman is Mary, and her seed is Christ. She was predestined from all eternity to be his mother and, appropriate divine preparations were not lacking. Were not the fruits of Christ's redemptive sacrifice (his Paschal Mystery) applied to her in anticipation; thereby preserving her from original sin and granting her fulness of grace. Such, we believe, is the meaning of her Immaculate Conception. The eighth chapter of the *Constitution on the Church* has as its heading: "The role of the Blessed Virgin Mary, Mother of God in the Mystery of Christ and the Church." What has it to say to us on this subject? "She is already prophetically foreshadowed in that victory over the serpent; she is the Virgin who is to conceive and bear a son, whose name will be called Emmanuel. She stands among the poor and humble of the Lord, who confidently await and receive salvation from him." [2] "The eternal Father willed that the consent of the predestined Mother should precede the Incarnation, so that just as a woman contributed to death so also a woman should contribute to life. . . By consenting, she became the Mother of Jesus. . . The Fathers of the Church see her used by God, not merely in a passive way, but as cooperating in the work of human salvation through free faith and obedience." [3] From the moment of Mary's consent onwards we cannot separate Mother and Child, Jesus and Mary. "This union of the Mother with her Son in the work of salvation was manifested," says the Council, "from the time of Christ's virginal conception to his death." [4] The document then goes on to give the scriptural events linking Jesus and Mary, from his birth to the cross. By that cross it says: "She stood, in keeping with the divine plan, suffering grievously with her only-begotten Son. There she united herself with a maternal heart to his sacrifice and lovingly consented to the immolation of this victim, which she herself had brought forth." [5] Her faith, her obedience, her love sustained her in her role and made her what she styled herself, "the handmaid of the Lord."

Tradition tells us that she was the first to enjoy the sight of the risen Christ. She was present too in the Cenacle at the first Pentecost, and she continued to be a mother to the infant Church by her prayers and her guidance. She is, as Pope Paul VI declared: "The Mother of the Church."

We know that "when her earthly sojourn was completed she was taken body and soul into heavenly glory and exalted by the Lord, her Son, as Queen of all, of heaven and earth, of angels and of men, so that she might be more thoroughly conformed to her Son, the conqueror of sin and death." Mary continues this her role from her throne in heaven the Council assures us. "She still exercises her maternal love and care for the brethren of her Son, her children, who still journey on earth until they too are led to their happy fatherland." The Council of course stresses the fact that Mary's role is subordinate to that of her Son and that she in no way adds anything to the dignity or takes away anything from the efficacy of Christ, the one Mediator. Mary has a special place in the Church when it re-lives the Paschal Mystery. In his Apostolic Letter, *Marialis Cultus*, of February 2nd 1974, Pope Paul VI deals with this matter. A brief summary of his teaching will be of interest at this point. The Pope wishes to offer considerations and directives concerning the relationship between the sacred liturgy and devotion to Our Lady, in order to help us develop "true devotion to the Mother of God". The Letter takes us through the liturgical year. Starting with Advent it shows us the place Mary occupies in that season. As he so often stresses she is always with Christ, as she was in their lives together on earth. He points out the special place Mary has in the Advent-Christmas liturgy.

He makes special mention of the new feast of the Divine Maternity on January 1st, which he says "commemorates the part played by Mary in the mystery of salvation and is intended to exalt the singular dignity which this mystery brings to the Mother, through whom we were found worthy to receive the author of life."

The Pope then speaks of the two solemnities of the Annunciation of the Lord and the Assumption of our Blessed Lady. "Both east and west," he says, "celebrate this solemnity of the Annunciation as the commemoration of the salvific 'Fiat of the Incarnate Word', who, entering the world, said: "God, here I am, I am coming to obey your will" (Heb. 10:7; Psalm 39). This feast commemorates the beginning of the redemption and the union of the divine nature with human nature in the one person of the Word. **The liturgy of this feast also sees Our Lady as the 'New Eve',** the obedient Virgin who with her generous 'Fiat' became, through the working of the Holy Spirit, the Mother of God. It celebrates her free consent and co-operation in the plan of redemption. The feast is as a joint one of Christ and Mary, one of the Word who becomes the Son of Mary and of the Virgin who becomes the Mother of God.

We contemplate her Assumption as her destiny attained in the fulness of the glory of her immaculate soul and virginal body, of her perfect conformity to the risen Christ. The **Holy Father adds: "this solemnity is prolonged in the feast of** her Queenship" (August 22nd). He tells us that "these four solemnities (Immaculate Conception, Divine Maternity, Annunciation and Assumption), marked with the highest liturgical rank, have regard to the main dogmatic truths concerning the handmaid of the Lord." He passes on to reflect on other feasts of Our Lady, "that commemorate salvific events in which the Blessed Virgin Mary was closely associated with her Son." He mentions her Nativity, the dawn of salvation, the morning star; the Visitation, when Our Lady brought graces and blessings to the home and parents of John the Baptist and to St. John himself. This occasion is recalled each day at Evening Prayer when the Church chants and makes her own the canticle of Our Lady, the 'Magnificat'. Attention is directed next to the Feast of Our Lady's Sorrows on September 15th and to that of the Presentation in the Temple (February 2nd) another joint feast of the Son and the Mother.

Other feasts of lesser rank are also recalled, and finally the Pope speaks of local feasts, i.e., those celebrated in certain places or in Religious Orders. He treats of the place Our

Lady holds in the new Roman Missal, e.g., Our Lady on Saturday, the special Prefaces in her honour, the mention of her in the Eucharistic Prayers, which have a paschal note. He draws our attention to the many passages in the *Lectionary* referring to Our Lady. He glances at other liturgical books and finds Mary has a prominent place, e.g., in the rite of baptism the Church invokes her, the Mother of grace; the Church invokes her intercession for mothers, who full of gratitude for the gift of motherhood, come to church to express their joy; the Church holds up Our Lady as a model to those who follow Christ by embracing the religious life; the Church prays fervently on behalf of her children who have come to the hour of their death, and also for those who have closed their eyes to the light of this world and appeared before Christ, the eternal Light. The Pope passes on to examine more closely the thought of Mary as a model of the spiritual attitude with which the Church celebrates and lives the divine mysteries in the liturgy. He treats it under four headings: *(1) Mary is the attentive Virgin*; this above all by her faith. "The Church also acts in this way, especially in the liturgy, when with faith she listens, accepts, proclaims and venerates the Word of God"; *(2) Mary is also the Virgin in prayer*; she appears as such in her 'Magnificat', at Cana in her petition to her Son. Here we have the prayer of praise, gratitude and petition. The last event recorded in the sacred Scriptures in Mary's life is again one of prayer; she is absorbed in prayer in the Cenacle, awaiting the Holy Spirit. Now that she has gone to heaven, she has not abandoned her mission of interceding for her children on earth; *(3) Mary is also the Virgin-Mother*. Her miraculous motherhood is an exemplar of the Virgin-Church who becomes herself a Mother, begetting children for the Kingdom of God in the waters of baptism. This links Mary with baptism. The early Fathers taught that the Church prolongs in the sacrament of baptism the virginal motherhood of Mary. Saint Leo says: "The origin which Christ took in the womb of the Virgin, he has given to the baptismal font." *(4) Mary is finally the Virgin presenting offerings.* Here the Pope reflects on the Presentation in the temple, and on Mary at Calvary, and shows the link with the liturgy; the first with the feast on February 2nd. and the second with every Mass. Just as Mary then shared in a most intimate way in the historical Mystery of Christ (his Paschal Mystery), so now she enters into its renewal in the life of the Church, and is a model for us in celebrating the renewal of the Paschal Mystery and partaking of its fruits in the various functions of the liturgy. Pope Paul selects two exercises of marian piety, the *Angelus* and the *Rosary* and he draws our attention to them from a liturgical point of view. The first he says reminds us of the Paschal Mystery, for we pray that we may be led through Christ's passion and death to the glory of his resurrection. He speaks at length about the Rosary, and shows its gospel inspiration. He calls it "a gospel of prayer", centred on the mystery of the redemptive incarnation. "It has been emphasised that the Rosary is, as it were, a branch sprung from the ancient trunk of the Christian Liturgy, the Psalter of Mary. It is not part of the liturgy but an aid to familiarise the faithful with the 'Mystery of Christ'." There is no grace that we can ask through Mary's intercession more fruitful than to ask her to help us share in the Mystery of her Son and so to live the Paschal Mystery in our own lives.

1. C.L. 103.
2. C.Ch. 55.
3. idem. 56.
4. idem. 57.
5. idem. 58.

8. THE PASCHAL MYSTERY AND THE SAINTS

In its chapter on the Liturgical Year the *Constitution on the Sacred Liturgy* treats of the saints and the Paschal Mystery. It says: "The Church has also included in the annual cycle, days devoted to the memory of her martyrs and her other saints... by celebrating the passage of these saints from earth to heaven the Church proclaims the Paschal Mystery achieved in those who have suffered and been glorified with Christ; she proposes them to the faithful as examples drawing all to the Father through Christ. . . The feasts of the saints proclaim the wonderful works of Christ in his servants and display to the faithful fitting examples for their imitation... Raised up to perfection by the manifold grace of God and already in possession of eternal salvation, they sing God's perfect praise in heaven and offer prayers for us." [1] In those words the link between the Paschal Mystery and the saints is clear. It shows us the fruits of the Mystery of Christ in their lives and their present sharing in the glory of heaven. Therefore we do not look at the saints in isolation but as people who have participated in the Paschal Mystery of Christ, who have lived that Mystery in their own lives here below and now share in the glory of their Head. They are now members of the Church Triumphant.

The saints present a challenge to us, and their victory gives us hope, and the confidence that where they are now in glory we too shall be, if like them we live out the Paschal Mystery in our own lives. These are two aspects of the feasts of the saints that we can look at; their lives while in the Church Militant here on earth, and their present lives in the Church Triumphant.

Like all of us the saints were initiated into the supernatural life in the waters of baptism. Their lives show us how they developed that new, divine life received at baptism.

The third Eucharistic Prayer opens with the words: "Father, . . .All life, all holiness comes from you through your Son, Jesus Christ our Lord." We cannot say that such a life is not for us, or not possible for us. Saint Paul answers such an attitude of negativity: "He (Father) chose us in Christ that we should be holy. . . who has predestined us into the adoption of children through Jesus Christ. . . unto the praise of the glory of his grace" (Eph. 1:4-6). St. Paul also says: "We are made rich in him so that there is not wanting to us in any grace" (1 Cor. 1:7). Christ himself had revealed the same to St. Paul himself when he felt his weakness most keenly: "My grace is sufficient for you" (2 Cor. 12:9).

Holiness then is not of our making. It is a sharing in the holiness of Christ. Do we not say in the 'Glory' of the Mass: "You alone are Holy." To live out their lives in holiness the saints were in constant contact with Christ and the mystery of his death and resurrection. This they maintained through the Mass, the sacraments, their daily spiritual exercises, and loyalty to their particular vocation in life. No saints fully realised in their lives all the aspects of that Mystery; one saint is outstanding in one way, another in another. *Mediator Dei* says: "In the virtues of the saints the virtue of Jesus Christ is variously reflected, and we must imitate them as they imitated Christ. In some we see apostolic zeal, in others an heroic fortitude, in some a constant watchfulness in expectation of the Redeemer, in others a virginal purity of soul and the gracious modesty of Christian humility, and in all a burning love for God and their neighbour. All these gems of holiness are set before our eyes by the liturgy, that we may gaze upon them with profit to our souls and be set on fire by their example." [2]

This aspect is again treated of in the *Constitution of the Church* in chapter 5: "On the call of the whole Church to holiness." There we can read: "It is evident that all the faithful of Christ of whatever rank or status are called to the fulness of the Christian life and to the perfection of charity... In order that the faithful may reach their perfection, they must use their strength according as they have received it, as a gift of God. In this way they can follow in his footsteps and mould themselves to his image, seeking the will of the Father in all things. . . In the various types and duties of life one and the same holiness is cultivated by all." The *Constitution* treats of this variety of vocations, all of which are sources of sanctification. It concludes: "All of Christ's faithful, therefore whatever be the conditions, duties and circumstances of their lives, will grow in holiness day by day through those various situations." It mentions some of the means available to anyone. "Each must share frequently in the sacraments, the eucharist especially, and in the liturgical rites. Each must apply himself constantly to prayer, self-denial, active brotherly service and the exercise of all the virtues." Thus we see all of Christ's followers are invited, are encouraged, and are bound to pursue holiness of life, and the perfect fulfilment of their proper state. Reflecting on the lives of the saints, the *Constitution on the Sacred Liturgy* not only reviews their participation in the Paschal Mystery on earth, but also their sharing in its triumph hereafter. The Prefaces in the New *Roman Missal* for various classes of saints join the two thoughts. Each Mass also recalls their glory: "Venerating the memory of the saints. . . we hope for some part and fellowship with them." The *Constitution* also says: "In the earthly liturgy we take part in a foretaste of that heavenly liturgy which is celebrated in the holy city of Jerusalem, towards which we journey as pilgrims. . . we sing a hymn to the Lord's glory with all the warriors of the heavenly army." [(3)] The *Constitution on the Church* raises our hearts, and our hopes, to the ultimate goal of all our striving. It says: "The Church to which we are called in Christ Jesus, and in which we acquire sanctity through the grace of God, will attain her full perfection only in the glory of heaven." [(4)] It points to the link binding the Church Militant, the pilgrim Church, with the Church Triumphant in heaven, and speaks of that union especially in the sacred liturgy: "Celebrating the eucharistic sacrifice (Christ's Paschal Mystery) we are most closely united to the worshipping Church in heaven as we join with and venerate the memory first of the glorious ever Virgin Mary, of Blessed Joseph and the blessed apostles and martyrs and of all the saints." [(5)]

In case we might still feel that holiness of life is only for the chosen few, the words of the Apocalypse used in the Mass for the feast of *All Saints* assure us that such is not the case: "I saw a great multitude which no man could number, of all nations and tribes and peoples and tongues, standing before the throne and in the sight of the Lamb, clothed in white robes and palms in their hands" (Apoc. 7:9-10). The completion of the Paschal Mystery in the saints is a source of hope and confidence for us who are still pilgrims, that one day we will be with them in glory to join with them in praising the Lamb who was slain and redeemed us in his blood.

Finally our close union with the Church Triumphant encourages us to invoke the intercession of the saints in our needs, to help us by their prayers. "They offer prayers for us," the *Constitution* states emphatically. All those thoughts are summed up in the doctrine of the Communion of Saints. The *Constitution* very clearly shows us what true devotion to the saints means. There is nothing sentimental about it. If we view the saints in the light of the Paschal Mystery (as the

153

Constitution does) we will see them for what they were and for what they are now, faithful followers of Christ here on earth and joint-heirs with him in glory.

1. C.L. 104.
2. M.D. 179.
3. C.L. 8.
4. C.Ch. 48.
5. idem. 50.

9. THE PASCHAL MYSTERY IN DAILY LIFE

We saw the importance of the Paschal Mystery in the lives of the saints. We have to learn to realise its importance in our own daily lives. We should not regard it as something outside ourselves. As it was for the saints, so it is for us, not just a model but a source of grace to enable us to live that mystery in everyday life. The final scene in the life of Christ on Calvary was, as he described it beforehand, like seed falling into the ground. He was dying in order to give birth to a new and full life with the Father.

Now we have died with Christ in baptism and risen with him to share in his risen life, which will only reach its maturity in the future life of glory. To maintain, to strengthen and to bring to perfection the Paschal Mystery in our everyday life we have to practise virtues of many kinds, theological and moral. We must not look on ascetical exercises in isolation, but as the living out in daily life of the Mystery of Christ, which is one of continual death to sin and to self, so that Christ may live and reign in us. Saint Paul writes of the ascetical life in the context of a continual death to sin as a result of baptism. But he sees the positive side of that constant dying, in the practice of the virtues.

Another aspect of the Mystery of Christ in our lives is our relationship with our neighbour. Christ was not only the suffering servant of the Father but also of his fellow-men:

"Greater love than this no man hath than to lay down his life for his friends" (Jn. 15:13). That aspect must find a place in our lives, and in our living of the Paschal Mystery. This will call, on our part, for constant self-sacrifice, self-giving, generosity and ministering charity. These daily challenges must be seen in the light of the Paschal Mystery.

When we turn to the *Constitution on the Sacred Liturgy* we find all of this explained to us: "The spiritual life is not limited, by any means, solely to participation in the liturgy. The Christian is indeed called to pray with his brethren, but he must also enter into his chamber to pray to the Father in secret; yet more, according to the teaching of the apostle, he should pray without ceasing. We learn from the same apostle that we must bear about in our body the dying of Jesus so that the life also of Jesus may be made manifest in our bodily frame." [1] "Popular devotions of the Christian people are to be highly recommended. . . But these devotions should be so drawn up that they harmonize with the liturgical seasons, accord with the sacred liturgy [2]. . . Finally, at various times of the year and according to traditional methods of training, the Church completes the formation of the faithful by means of pious practices for soul and body, by instruction, prayer and works of penance and of mercy." [3] The Church sees our whole lifetime, from baptism onwards, as a sharing in, and entering into, Christ's Paschal Mystery. The mystery of death and resurrection will give unity to our Christian way of life.

What then is it that makes Christ's Paschal Mystery the focal point in our lives? Is it that he redeemed us, paid our debt for sin? Yes, but there is more than that. It was God's second start, as it were, in forming mankind according to his divine plan. Recall the words of St. Leo (used in the former rite of the Mass) "O God, who in a marvellous manner created and ennobled man's being, and in a manner still more marvellous you renewed it." St. John says: "He (Christ) was full of grace and of his fulness we have all received, grace for grace" (Jn. 1:16). St. Paul sees in our new life, a new creation, making us a new creature. The basis for new hope and new victory is in Christ. However, to maintain, increase and safeguard this new divine life given us in baptism, we must, according to the teaching of St. Paul be prepared 'to crucify our flesh and its vices' (Gal. 5:24), and "cast off the old man" (Col. 3:9). This is necessary "that we may grow unto the fulness of Christ" (Eph. 4:13), so that we may be able to say: "For me to live is Christ" (Ph. 1:21), and "I live now, not I, but Christ lives in me" (Gal. 2:20). The one object of practising the virtues is to deepen and perfect the Paschal Mystery in us. It is indeed the full acceptance of Christ's invitation to deny ourselves, to take up our cross daily, to follow him, to become like him. He humbled himself, he became obedient, he was merciful, forgiving, he was patient and kind, he was unselfish and thoughtful of others, he was prayerful but active in the service of others. His love was truly sacrificial. In reality he could say: "Come follow me" (Matt. 4:19), "I am the way, the truth and the life" (Jn. 14:6), "Learn of me" (Matt. 11:29), and "I have given you an example" (Jn. 13:15). The *Instruction on the implementation of the Constitution on the Liturgy* sums all that up for us in the words: "The Christian life expresses the Paschal Mystery in which the Son of God, incarnate and made obedient even unto death, is so exalted in his resurrection and ascension that he may share his divine life with the world. By this life, men, dead to sin and conformed to Christ, may live no longer for themselves but for him who died for them and rose again. This is done through faith in Christ and through the sacraments, chiefly through baptism and the most sacred mystery of the eucharist". The Council had clearly stated that the grace of the sacraments "flows from the Paschal Mystery, the very font from which they draw their power." [4] The other Council Documents also exhort the faithful to develop the spirit and practice of prayer, by drawing on the authentic sources of spirituality.

They recommend the reading of the Sacred Scriptures and meditation on them, so as to attain the "excellent knowledge of Christ".

No one else has developed the theology of the Christian life as did St. Paul in his inspired writings. He teaches, corrects, exhorts, and all the time he does so in the light of the Paschal Mystery. He asks: "How can we who died to sin still live in it?" (Rm. 6:2). Over and over again he stresses this constant need to die to sin, to put to death all that is earthly in us. But he emphasizes the positive side as well. He tells us that we must "walk in newness of life" (Rm. 3:4). "If we have been raised up with Christ we must seek the things that are above, not the things on earth" (Col. 3:1-2); "You must consider yourself dead to sin and alive in Christ" (Rm. 6:11); "Whoever is led by the Spirit of God are the sons of God" (Rm. 8:14).

He gives us a picture of his own soul and its progress in his letter to the Philippians (chapter 3): "All I want to know is Christ and the power of his resurrection and to share in his sufferings, by reproducing *the pattern of his death*." How paschal those words are. He sees his life as a constant struggle but he shows his great confidence, "Not as though I were already perfect. . . forgetting the things that are behind and stretching forth myself to those that are before, I press forward towards the mark, to the prize of the supernal vocation of God in Christ Jesus. . . Be ye followers of me as I am of Christ" (Ph. 3:12 ff). One can go still deeper and recall that at baptism we received the three theological virtues not to lie dormant. Their exercise is essential for developing our Christian life. One of the Sunday prayers begs for an increase of those three virtues. Faith is so fundamental, that without an active and lively faith nothing else has any meaning. Without this faith our Christian life becomes empty. Hope is likewise necessary, because we know that of ourselves we can do nothing in the supernatural order. We must have constant trust and confidence in the mercy and merits of Christ, won for us in his Paschal Mystery. Again St. Paul gives us wonderful example and encouragement when treating of the value of those virtues for our Christian lives. It is he too who reminds us that Charity, love of God, has been poured into our hearts by the Holy Spirit who has been given us. St. Paul does not divide our lives into compartments, but sees everything as leading us to union with the Father in and through Christ. He has outlined it all for us as a continual dying with Christ, rising with Christ, sitting in high places with Christ. He sees Christ as his very life: "for me to live is Christ" (Ph. 1:21). He sees our Christian life as nothing else than the reality of the unfolding of the Paschal Mystery in our daily lives. All spirituality has its origin in the Paschal Mystery. Each school emphasises one or other aspect but all aim at forming Christ in the soul. It is worth recalling the words of Pope Pius XI on this subject: "The liturgy is not the school of this or that party but the school of the Church." Pius XII said: "The piety which is derived from the sacred liturgy possesses the greatest efficacy for the spiritual lives of all Christians and for each individual soul." [5] It is in that spirit that the Church prays on the first Sunday of Lent: "Deepen our understanding of the mystery of Christ and make it a reality in the conduct of our lives."

---

1. C.L. 12.
2. idem. 13.
3. idem. 105.
4. idem. 61.
5. Letter to a liturgical congress in Spain.

10. THE PASCHAL MYSTERY AND DEATH

Death is the final unfolding of the Paschal Mystery in our Christian life. It is a real sharing in Christ's own death, a sharing that leads to a new life, that will last for ever with the Father. Here as in all things else "he has given us an example" (Jn. 13:15). From our *Creed* we know that Christ died and how he died; "He suffered under Pontius Pilate, was crucified, died and was buried," but we also add, "The third day he rose from the dead." How did Christ face death? Like all of us he feared it, as is clear from his agony in the garden. Yet he overcame this natural fear and said: "Not my will but thine be done" (Mk. 14:36). In his bitter Passion we see him go through it all with patience and fortitude, and at the end cry out: "Father into thy hands I commend my spirit" (Lk. 23:46), before bowing his head and dying. In life he confronted death, and on at least three occasions he raised dead people to life. Before he called Lazarus from the tomb he said: "I am the resurrection and the life" (Jn. 11:25). Christ teaches us to accept death in union with his own death and in atonement for our sins. St. Paul has many things to say about our death and resurrection, but always in reference to Christ's own death and resurrection (cfr. the readings from St. Paul in the masses for the dead). He sees our victory over death as a sharing in Christ's own victory: "Thanks be to God who has given us the victory through our Lord Jesus Christ" (1 Cor. 15:17), and again

"When Christ will appear, who is your life, then you also shall appear with him in glory" (Col. 3:4), or: "Behold I tell you a mystery we shall all indeed rise again" (1 Cor. 15:51). We must not forget the food that Christ has prepared for our journey through death, our passing from time to eternity. That food is *Holy Viaticum*. It is the sacrament of the dying. It too recalls the Paschal Mystery: Christ becomes our companion in that last journey. He who has provided for every stage along the road of life has not forgotten to provide strength and help for those vital final moments. The *Constitution on the Sacred Liturgy* has all this in mind when it says: "The Rite for the burial of the dead should express more clearly the Paschal character of Christian death." [1] In the *Decree* introducing the new Rite we read: "In celebrating the funeral rites Christians should certainly affirm their hope in eternal life. It has been the Church's custom in the funeral rites not only to commend the dead to God, but also to support the Christian hope of the people, and give witness to its faith in the future resurrection of the baptised in Christ. For this reason the *Constitution on the Sacred Liturgy* directed that the funeral rites be revised to express more clearly the *paschal* character of Christian death." The opening words of the new Rite itself express the same thought: "In the funeral rites the Church celebrates the Paschal Mystery of Christ. Those who in baptism have become one with the dead and risen Christ will pass with him from death to life, to be purified in soul and welcomed into the fellowship of the saints in heaven. . . The Church therefore celebrates the eucharistic sacrifice of Christ's Passover for the dead." Those thoughts linking death and resurrection with Christ's Paschal Mystery find ample expression in the new Rite. The scripture readings are chosen to proclaim the Paschal Mystery. In the variety of prayers, hope in the life to come is enkindled in the Christian: e.g., "Lord God, your Son redeemed us by dying and rising to life again. Since our brother (sister) believed in

161

the mystery of our own resurrection, let him (her) share the joys and blessings of the life to come." The Mass, which is the renewal of the Paschal Mystery, is the very centre of the whole Rite. Its special readings and prayers are chosen to strengthen our faith and hope in a future life. The *Prayers of the Faithful* follow the same theme. The first of the variety of Prefaces gives us the true Christian outlook on death:' "We who are saddened by the certain need to die may be consoled, for when the home of this earthly life is dissolved, an everlasting dwelling in heaven shall be gained." The Mass is followed by what is styled "The final commendation and farewell." This indeed is most consoling for the bereaved. Listen to some of it: "May, Christ, the Good Shepherd lead him (her) safely home to be at peace with God our Father... Saints of God, come to his (her) aid. Come to meet him (her) angels of the Lord. . . May Christ who called you take him (her) to himself. . . May the angels lead you into paradise, may the martyrs welcome you and take you to the holy city, the new and eternal Jerusalem. May the choirs of angels welcome you. Where Lazarus is poor no longer, may you have eternal rest. I am the resurrection and the life. The man who believes in me will live even if he dies and every living person who puts faith in me will never suffer eternal death." The final prayers at the grave are also consoling: "Lord Jesus Christ, by the three days you lay in the tomb you made holy the graves of all who believe in you. . . Give our brother (sister) peaceful rest in this grave, until that day when you, the resurrection and the life, will raise him (her) up in glory." Again *Prayers of the Faithful* are recited and the concluding prayer is a final plea that God in his love and mercy will give the deceased a place with his angels and saints. One more interesting point worth mentioning is that the Paschal Candle should be lighted at the head of the coffin, reminding us that Christ, the light of the world, gave us the light of faith at baptism (symbolised by the lighted candle given us) will now light the way through the dark

162

passage (passover) into the brightness of eternal light and life.

The funeral rite is not the end. Mother Church still remembers and prays for her departed children. This she does in every mass, in the *Memento for the Dead*. She celebrates regular anniversary masses. Each year she celebrates a feast for all her dead, on November 2nd. That month is dedicated to the memory of the Holy Souls. All this should bring home to us the doctrine of the Church Suffering, even after death; they are part of the Communion of Saints and we have fraternal and community obligations to them.

1. C.L. 81.

11. CONCLUSION

On the last Sunday of the Liturgical Year the Church celebrates a feast in honour of the *Kingship of Christ*. This feast is the climax of the celebration during the year of the Mystery of Christ under its various aspects. Sacred Scripture is very clear about this doctrine of the Kingship of Christ. The fact of his kingship was foretold in the Old Testament. But the chosen people came to see their future Messiah as an earthly king with an earthly kingdom who would liberate them from all foreign domination. Such was not to be for he said: "My kingdom is not of this world" (Jn. 18:36). His kingship was announced to our Blessed Lady and proclaimed by the Magi. During his public life the people tried, on two occasions, to make him king. They also proclaimed him king on his triumphal entry into Jerusalem before his Passion. His kingship was the chief cause for his death. This is very clear from St. John's story of the Passion. Pilate upheld this claim of Christ in the inscription he had placed over the Cross. It is important to realize that the claim to kingship was no mere claim to a title of honour. Christ was king by divine right because of his divinity. He was king by conquest for he ransomed the souls of men from the kingdom of darkness for the kingdom of light, from the kingdom of death for the kingdom of life, from the kingdom of Satan for the kingdom of God. During the year the Liturgy keeps this image of Christ as King always before us. The *Advent* Liturgy pictures his coming as the Messiah-King. He is greeted at Christmas as "The Prince of Peace", "Our King and Lawgiver," "King of the Gentiles." The Epiphany is in reality a feast of his Kingship. The Liturgy of *Holy Week* has many references to his Kingship. The blessing and procession of the palms on *Palm Sunday* are our homage to Christ, our King. His Kingship is mentioned in the narration of the Passion. The veneration of the Cross on *Good Friday* sees him as the victorious King, who reigned from the Cross. The *Paschal Vigil*, and the season of *Paschaltime*, celebrate this victory of our King and Lord over the powers of evil. Throughout the liturgical year then the Kingship of Christ is almost always viewed in the light of his Paschal Mystery. The feast of his Kingship on the final Sunday of the Church's Year of grace is a celebration in anticipation of that *grande finale* when, at the end of time, Christ will appear in glory, in power, and in majesty, to take possession of his victorious kingdom and hand it over to his Father. That will be the day of the glorious resurrection from death, when the dead will rise from their graves to go and share, in body and soul, the glory of the Father's kingdom, to become joint-heirs with Christ in the Church Triumphant. That will be the completion of the working out of the Paschal Mystery in Christ's Mystical Body, his Church. Then the elect will join in the eternal canticle to the Lamb that was slain and has redeemed us in his blood. That will be the final chapter in the story of salvation-history, in which we all have figured. This thought echoes again what we said at the very start: "God is love" (1 Jn. 4:16), "God so loved the world that he sent his only beloved Son that all who believe in him might have eternal life" (Jn. 3:16), "the love of God has been poured into our hearts by the Holy Spirit who has been given us" (Rm. 5:51). We have seen the concrete proof of this. The working out of that divine plan of love has centred around the Paschal Mystery; with its preparatory stage in the Old Testament, its realisation in Christ's redemptive work and in its application to each succeeding generation through the Church's liturgy, reliving in her members that Paschal Mystery. It will find its completion in the heavenly liturgy where as *Mediator Dei* puts it: "We will reach that inner sanctuary beyond the veil, there to honour our heavenly Father for all eternity." [1] The *Constitution on the Sacred Liturgy* sees in our earthly liturgy "a foretaste of that heavenly liturgy which is celebrated in the holy city of Jerusalem towards which we journey as pilgrims. . . we eagerly await our saviour, the Lord Jesus Christ, until he, our life, shall appear and we too will appear with him in glory." [2]

1. M.D. 182.
2. C.L. 8.

BIBLIOGRAPHY

Mediator Dei. . . Encyclical of Pius XII on the Liturgy, (1947).

Constitution on the Sacred Liturgy, Vatican II.

Theological Dimensions of the Liturgy, Cyprian Vagagini O.S.B., Liturgical Press, Collegeville U.S.A. (1959).

Liturgy and Spirituality, Gabriel M. Braso O.S.B., Collegeville, U.S.A. (1959).

A commentary on the Prefaces and Eucharistic Prayers of the Roman Missal, Mgr. Soubegou, translated by Rev. J.A. Otto. Collegeville, U.S.A. (1971).

The Liturgy of Vatican II (2 vols.), edited by W. Baruna, translated by Jovian Lang O.F.M., Franciscan Herald Press, Chicago (1966).

Eucharist, Louis Bouyer, Notre Dame Press, U.S.A. (1968).

Life & Liturgy, Louis Bouyer, Sheed & Ward, (1954).

The Paschal Mystery in Parish Life, Henri Oster, translated by M.C. O'Brien, Burns & Oates/Herder (1967).

The Sacraments of Life & Worship, J.P. Sachanz, Geoffrey Chapman (1967).

The Bible & the Liturgy, Jean Danielou S.J., Darton, Longman & Todd, (1956).

Introduction to the Liturgy, Ambrosius Verheul, Anthony Clarke Books, England, (1972).

The New Liturgy, Edited by L. Sheppherd, Darton, Longman (1970).

Pastoral Liturgy, A Symposium, Edited by Harold Winston, Collins, (1975).

The Mass & the People of God, J.D. Crichton, Burns & Oates, (1966).

Christian Celebration of the Mass, J.D. Crichton, (1971).

Christian Celebration of the Sacraments, J.D. Crichton, Chapman (1973).

Christian Celebration. . . Prayer, J.D. Crichton, Chapman, (1976).

The Ministry of Reconciliation, J.D. Crichton, Chapman, (1974).

The Liturgy of the Hours with Commentary, by A.M. Roguet O.P., Chapman, (1971).

Christ in His Mysteries, Dom Columba Marmion O.S.B., (Sandes).

The Mass of the Roman Rite (2 Vols.), Joseph J. Jungmann S.J., (Benziger), (1950).

Advent to Epiphany, Lent & Holy Week, Pasch to Pentecost, Vincent Ryan O.S.B., Veritas, Dublin, (1977).

Printed in Ireland by the Society of St. Paul, Athlone